How to Survive in America
A Ten-Step Guide

Ian C. Dawkins Moore

OTHER BOOKS BY I.C. DAWKINS MOORE

Blame it on Reno – a comedy story & screenplay

How to Survive in America – a ten step guide

Maili Beach – a noir novella

You Can't Push a String Up a Hill – short stories

The Alchemy of Happiness – a comedy novella

The Rituals for Success – a self-help book

The Arrival: how to survive in America – essays

Divine Providence – short stories and poems

American Charity – a novel

The Meaning of Life – short stories and poems

Return to My Native Land –travels in West Africa

Open Heart Poetry – poetry about love & loss

America: Culture Shock – essays on culture

Great Black Innovators – the art of problem solving

Afro-Muse: The Evolution of African-American Music

Culture Shock Essays – essays of cultural travels

Ian C. Dawkins Moore

HOW TO SURVIVE IN AMERICA

©Copyright 2015/2019 Ian C. Dawkins Moore

ISBN:13: 9781790572052

ALL RIGHTS RESERVED

ACKNOWLEDGMENTS:

To Sue Stoney for her diligent work editing and proof-reading this book.

To Jazmine Moore for the beautiful cover artwork and to my wife Bridgette whose support through the years has allowed me to write these essays.

In courtesy of:
- *Brit-Think, Ameri-Think* – Penguin copyright©1986 Jane Walmsley
- *Riding the Waves of Culture – Understanding Diversity in Global Business* – copyright©1998 Fons Trompenaars & Charles Hampden-Turner
- "Let America Be America Again" – copyright©1935 Langston Hughes
- "Mud bone" by See Richard Pryor ***

I am solely responsible for the selections and articles in this book.

Ian C. Dawkins Moore

DEDICATION

To all who would venture to these shores...

The bitterness of poor quality remains long after the sweetness of low price is forgotten.
~Benjamin Franklin

CONTENT:

Step One - Coming to America	8
Step Two - The 7 Phases of Surviving Culture Shock	14
Step Three - How to Be an American (with a Tip of My Hat to Jane Walmsley & a Big Shovel Full of Irony and Sarcasm)	18
Step Four - ESL (Or English as a Stupid Language)	27
Step Five – Only in America	34
Step Six - The Art of Communicating	48
Step Seven - Getting a Job	54
Step Eight - How to Give a Speech	70
Step Nine - Tomorrow Belongs to the Communicators	77
Step Ten - The Culture of Survival	80
Let America be America Again by Langston Hughes	95
About the Author: Ian C. Dawkins Moore	98
Workshops with IDMoore Consulting	100
Other Books by Ian C. Dawkins Moore	102

THE ARRIVAL

And I came—naked—
free!
Burned by destiny's
anthem
yet cloistered by the fire of
my desire spitting
hopes out towards the horizons
that shrunk away
from my tremendous commitment
to suck up all my
disappointments
and mistakes and imbibe them
with the pregnancy
of a new birthing!
Come then
into this fire of
cleansing power,
burn away the
warts of transgressions
and fears. Embrace
this silent hour
of our arrival—
here, brother,
sip cool waters.

Step One – COMING TO AMERICA

COMING TO AMERICA

> *Ships coming from a distance carry everyone's dreams ashore. For some, they slip in with the eddies of the tides. For others, they crash against the rocks of poor fortune. Each brings their new song of freedom, coming to America.*
> Zora Neale Hurston

When I first visited New York and stumbled over the stacks of garbage on the corner of Fifth Avenue, I was amazed by such poverty side-by-side with such wealth. I later discovered that the city was going broke; and that New Yorkers were betting on the city's demise. Years later, when I flew into San Francisco, I was greeted by quite the opposite spectacle.

My wife's sister picked us up in her 500 SL Mercedes and ferried us through a kaleidoscope of dazzling billboards advertising everything from gambling in sun-baked Reno to giving humanitarian aid to Darfur. I was deposited, after a ride across the elegant Bay Bridge, at Lake Merritt, the pride of Oakland's American-African bourgeoisie. I had to pinch myself to believe the opulence was real.

It was real. The American-African community of Oakland, California, is probably one of the wealthiest Black cities in the world. The skyline houses that look down from the redwood hills of the East Bay are not the exclusive preserve of whites, as is often the case in many neo-colonial lands. The sun-drenched Mediterranean climate is host to one of the most diverse communities in America. Yet beyond the mortar and bricks of their homes, American-Africans own very little of the wealth of this fertile region.

On my arrival in Oakland, California, I learned that the city was scorned by San Francisco, the city across the bay. Oakland's population used to be more than 60 percent American-African, but it has now shrunk to less than 35 percent. Yet the racial tag has stuck, and Oakland continues to be subjected to insinuations of second-class citizenship.

This abuse only serves to highlight the cruel irony of history; Oakland was the celebrated start of the Trans-Continental railway, which was built to bring Easterners to the gold of the Sierra Mountains. But the fame of the whoring town of 'Frisco had spread too wide for the truth to be known – that San Francisco was just a stop-over place for far more rewarding adventures elsewhere.

It was not, however, until I began to work with Americans that I got to see the people behind their facades. Stripped of a reason to care, people often don't. Settled people become addicted to their immediate gratifications, and their interest in others becomes disturbingly absent.

The American public persona being the embodiment of the perfect lifestyle is a veneer that fools nobody, least of all someone new to the country eager to dig beneath the surface with every question. American lifestyles are so tied to credit and debit – and an obsession with a crime – that to come to America is to feast on dreams of fabled opportunities and harsh, demoralizing realities.

My first encounter with Americana came after I pounded the streets for a month, looking for a position comparable to that of an engineer, which I'd been in London. I was told by an agency interviewer, in no uncertain terms, that as a Black man, I could not hope to get a position that would allow for upward mobility. I could only hope for lateral movement.

American racism strikes foreigners with such bold frankness that, on the first impression, it comes as a relief from the hypocrisy of the British class system. Yet the acceptance of conflicts among racial groups in America is so prevalent, and reveals an attitude of such bitterness, that it chokes every fiber of the nation's structure. All sides tug, push, and pull, using an ever-louder voice with which to express their mutual detachment.

Short of a nation undergoing a civil war, nowhere in the world is bitterness for one's fellow citizens such a fundamental part of the psyche of the country. Most startlingly, it is a bitterness that believes it's the most victimized in the world.

Trying to explain the 1,000-year conflict between Scotland and England to an American-African is to be reduced to a profound disconnect. American-Africans pride themselves on being history's most prominent victims, as if no other group – Black or white – could possibly have suffered so much!

I was finally saved from the grip of this consuming form of racism by the guiding hand of patronage; in the land of the brave and the free, it's not what you know but who you know! A cousin of my wife just happened to be on the local school board. He found me a job as a janitor at a junior college where I eventually worked for four years.

During my apprenticeship, I was exposed to American-African supervisors who took more than two years to summon the nerve to have a conversation with me beyond, "What's 'appenin'?" It took me some time to realize that, as a Black Englishman, I frustrated most Americans I met because

I didn't fit into a neat box (i.e., White, Black, Asian, Hispanic or Other).

This confusion I was causing reminded me of when I first filled out a visa form to come to the USA; I had to grapple with questions that asked me what my grandparents' ancestry and religion were. And whether I or any of my distant relatives, had committed a crime for which we weren't convicted. And finally, what was my race? I resisted this attempt to be made into a racist as long as I could, but I was encouraged and indeed impelled by the attitudes of American bureaucracy to view myself in this one-dimensional manner.

Try as I might; however, my accent set me apart, and my attitude really seemed to upset my supervisors so much so that they were always finding ways to mess with me. In social interactions, too, my accent drew attention. As a result, I was subjected to a wide range of responses – from people staring at me, mouths opened in disbelief, who then stormed out of the room muttering, "Who is that nigger?" to women approaching me and asking me to, "Just say som'thang." The former I lost no sleep over. The latter I learned to live with.

After these teething-times of acculturation, a process that everyone goes through in learning another culture, I was swept up by the vibrancy of American-African life in Oakland. The bubbly familiarity of American-Africans is an intoxicant to the newcomer, mainly when that newcomer has come from a European tradition that considers any display of emotions to be "uncivilized." For a Black man who had lived in isolation and cultural persecution in England, America represented a land flowing with milk and honey.

Seeing prosperous Black people strolling the streets was enough to get my heart pumping with feelings of pride and self-worth. The daily acknowledgment of American-Africans for each other in the streets introduced me to a brotherhood I'd not known before. The encouraging expressions of warmth in the language instilled an emotional bond that resurrected my wounded soul. It seemed to me that the American-African world of the East Bay was just a kiss away from paradise.

Yet as a Black individual who had also traveled and lived in Africa, I found my assimilation into American-African culture difficult. Firstly, because it seems to me that America binds all people of color to its knee-jerk fight for survival, without necessarily knowing what is in the best interest of a given individual; and, secondly, because American-Africans are blind to a global consciousness and alternative solutions to individual liberation.

For example, throughout the world, people of color understand that they are the victims of myriad discriminations. It is understood that those who do the discriminating (The Man, The Whites, Them, etc.) are themselves robbed of the one thing they seek to take from us – humanity.

When American-Africans play their game of hate and bitterness, they deliver up to their oppressors that which they seek and ensure their own slavery. Thus, when American-Africans use derogatory words to describe each other, they are not inventing a unique cultural language; instead, they are propagating the language of slavery.

Nothing disgusts a cultural African more than to hear an American-African refer to himself and his kinsman as a "nigga." This is no solution. Instead it is a papering over of the pain of humiliation, a sublimated denial of the self as a deserving, feeling, human being. It is also not a solution when educated American-Africans mimic ghetto-speak to impress their friends with just how "street" they are! It seems to me that respect and love for oneself must be the number one priority for many people. For people that have been enslaved both physically and mentally, respect and love must be pursued as a religious commitment.

I found it difficult settling into the American-African world because I made the mistake of thinking America would be just like Britain. "People speak English here; don't they?" For a foreigner, America's unique culture defies traditional social norms. While most countries are united by the sameness of their people, ideas, religion, and character, America defines itself – and is characterized by others – by its diversity.

The Anglo-Saxons may still control the corridors of power in America, but the pulse of the nation is in the explosive variety of its streets. It's as if it were a nation that's reaching for the sky, only to surrender.

Coming to America, the voyager is suspended between the dream of freedom – a freedom that offers credit to include everyone in the scheme of things – and the reality of slavery – slavery that compels conformity to debt.

America is freedom whose passion is out of control, but its very confusion is the catalyst that sparks excellent adventures. America is an emotion that claims objectivity, believing hopelessly in the intellectual rights of man. Yet as the real world of finite resources encroaches on America's glut of power, it will only be America's capacity for adaptability that promises it a special place in the world of the future.

STEP TWO - THE 7 PHASES OF SURVIVING CULTURE SHOCK

Someone who is going to live in another country will experience the cultural dislocation we call "culture shock." These are normal feelings of being helpless and frustrated in a new country where you may not speak the language or understand the culture.

But the new country can also feel like a love affair, in which you are exposed to lots of new and exciting thoughts and feelings. Here are the seven stages that most people go through in learning to integrate into their new homeland.

1 THE HONEYMOON
- Everything is beautiful.
- The weather is beautiful.
- The people are beautiful.
- The money is beautiful.
- I just don't understand anyone.

2   THE FIRST FIGHT
- This is not like it is at home.
- What will they think of next?
- Why do they do that?
- When will he stop talking?
- Where can I get an aspirin?

3   I'M IN LOVE AGAIN
- You know; if he just slowed down, I'd understand him.
- I can't believe I'm free.
- I could live here forever.
- The money's beautiful.
- Everything is beautiful.

4 *Sometimes I'm Up; Sometimes I'm Down*
- Why didn't I hear from home this week?
- Wow, that concert/ballgame was awesome!
- I wonder if they got the money order I sent them last week.
- It's great making real money!
- I know I shouldn't be so hard on myself.

5 *I need a Break*
- Too much stress. Too much new stuff.
- I really miss home.
- I'm glad I still have my hobby— playing the guitar.
- I finally found a support group with people just like me.
- KISS: Keep it simple, Silly!

6 *Learning the Language*
- Good means bad and bad means good?
- Back to school! There's lots of help here.
- Practice makes perfect.
- Slow down; success takes time—one step at a time.
- "Will you please repeat that again?"

7 *Becoming an American*
- Getting a job
- Learning the rules
- Joining groups
- Keeping up with my interests
- Getting to say what I really want

As a new American, you will feel a certain amount of frustration and irritability as you begin to learn about America. These tips will help you in your acculturation:

- Keep an open mind—things are not always what they seem.
- Ask questions.
- Don't rush to make judgments.
- Make every effort to learn to speak English as soon as possible.
- Be patient and try to understand American culture without criticizing it or comparing it to your own.
- Participate in American life. Americans love to join groups and give to charities. By doing so yourself, you will learn the language and the culture quickly if you try to meet Americans.
- Americans really like to be liked.
- Remember how far you have come, not how far you have to go.
- Get a job as soon as possible and make plans to improve, advance and succeed in the future.

VISITORS' OBSERVATIONS OF AMERICANS

The comments quoted in this section reflect the first impressions of individuals traveling to America from around the world and do not represent the governments or political positions of their countries.

Visitor from India:
-Americans are in a perpetual hurry; they don't allow themselves leisure time to enjoy life.

Visitor from Kenya:
-Americans are distant, not close to other Americans.
-Individualism is high.
-American students are restless, inattentive, rebellious, and the teachers have poor class discipline.

-Parents are too preoccupied with work and can't spend time with their kids.

Visitor from Ethiopia:
-Americans are direct. They want a YES or a NO answer and don't like it when you speak figuratively.

Visitor from Iran:
-Americans use the word "friend" loosely; it doesn't imply close ties or real bonds.

Visitor from Vietnam:
-Americans are handy, even women.
-Americans are friendlier to strangers but don't always care about family members.

Visitor from the Philippines:
-Children are very forward in their speaking. They have no respect for elders.
-Children don't offer help to their parents willingly. They either must be told or be rewarded with some kind of compensation.

Visitor from Korea:
-Teachers give students too many choices, even for the kind of assignment to do. And the students still don't do well.

STEP THREE –HOW TO BE AN AMERICAN
(WITH A TIP OF MY HAT TO JANE WALMSLEY AND A BIG SHOVEL FULL OF IRONY AND SARCASM)

The first thing you should know is what NOT to do. Don't do what I did. Don't assume that because Americans speak English, they understand English the way an English person speaks it, or in fact how others use English. As an ESL teacher, I realize that English is a language, but more importantly, America has a specific cultural approach to communication. The culture of the American style is as diverse as its people.

For all the red, white and blue flags that adorn people's homes across the country, most Americans have little in common with each other. Because America is a continent and not just a state, its geography is vastly different from the cold north of Alaska to the sweltering heat of the Gulf of Mexico, from the dry desert lands of the south and southwest to the bludgeoning concrete jungles of the northeast.

And that's before you meet the people—who are more diverse than their land. America emboldens people. America forces people to act as individuals. America incorporates every type of climate, and correspondingly, every kind of lifestyle and personality needed to live in such diverse communities. The idea that the United States is united is a misnomer. It exists precisely because it's not united and each state, county, region, city, town, and household acts like a law unto itself.

The second thing not to do is use irony, pathos, satire or sarcasm in your language with Americans. Americans take themselves very seriously—unless they're complete screw-ups, in which case they demand to be laughed at. Self-effacing humor is not appreciated. All humor and comedy are aimed at someone else, which is why the political incorrectness movement is so devastating to the political and social commentators who rely on stereotypes to simplify their explanations of the complexities of the world.

The observations in this book, consequently, will upset a lot of Americans who read them—and cause them to make it a hit because they will trash it or love it on social media. Either way, speaking the truth unsettles most Americans, its the price of having an honest and freedom-loving attitude.

The A#1 thing that people new to America need to understand is the concept of "Attitude." The noun is always used as a verb. "Attitude" is an action, both positive and negative, which colors your presentation to the world and defines you as someone to be reckoned with. "Attitude" can be summed up by the adage: "I'm gonna life forever," because Americans don't believe they are going to die—that only happens to the other guy.

Americans think that death is a choice. Therefore, to be truly worthy of your God-given right to be an American, your "Attitude" must be built on a deep-seated belief that you can delay death (or avoid it altogether) if you really try. So it's up to you; because if you die before your time, you'll have no one to blame but yourself.

This explains America's obsession with Dr. Oz, health shows, exercise, miracle supplements, plastic surgery, and talk shows that turn personal problems into entertainment. The basic concept of American life is that you've got just one life to live—although, with advances in medical science, there's an increasing possibility that you can replace parts that fall off your body— that, it's up to you to get it right the first time. Therefore, you must use your time purposefully and maximize your individual potential (have a nose job, get a college degree, marry rich) and grab as much money as possible.

The most significant "Attitude" you will need to cultivate is your view of yourself as a rock star, or porn star, or TV star! Talking about yourself in the third person (Queen E. of the UK has overused the "we" phrase), "Like" you are somebody, has a magical way of bringing attention to yourself. This is difficult for most people who come from "civilized" (self-referencing cultures) because self-advertisement smells of lack of self-worth and integrity.

Be that as it may, you will find it useful to develop a malleable schizophrenic character that finds no fault with pretentious, self-aggrandizing citizens who need to tell you about themselves. Think of it as a new way to learn patience and understanding like one of those '60's hippy songs.

I digress—the last paragraph was only about Californians (and wannabe Californians)—the ones everyone in the rest of America thinks are KooKoo! So, let me return to talking about taking care of your body. It's essential that you cultivate an attitude that conveys the belief to those around you that you will live forever! Because that's what Americans believe. So, it's essential to be prepared for immortality.

When you see the sales in the paper, be on the look-out for the unique snake oil formula praised by some celebrity whose career was going down the toilet until he or she discovered a pill that gave that celebrity perfect health. It's only your faith in being in excellent health that protects you from the reality that at any moment you may become a ward of the state in one of its hospitals. Faith is everything!

"Attitude" is the critical illusion needed to believe in the optimism of being an American. Your life is only in your own hands if you believe it is! It's imperative that you block out all references to objective reality. This requires a strong self-centered attitude. "Attitude" has no class or racial distinction—everyone has an attitude in America.

You owe it to yourself to be beautiful, clever, skinny, prosperous, and healthy "with attitude"; and if you fail, it's because you're not trying hard enough. Death and poverty are not natural phenomena but rather the product of your own lack of ambition and self-centeredness.

Real Americans are the world's greatest believers in newness. Newness increases and gets better all the time—or it should. The daily thrill of discovering something new in advertisements is anticipation that starts the moment one wakes up and rises to a white-hot fever pitch of beatific excitement as the toxic sales rags come sluicing through your mailbox.

The good old days don't exist for a Real American— even the anti-Christ music styles of Rap and the overly special-effected action movies are considered better, because they're newer. Newness trumps quality. History is old and dead because it's not new. Modern medicine is better, newer and improved: Once there was smallpox; now there is Ebola—a new disease! Old things are treated with distrust— as signs of poverty!

Real Americans know better, funnier and newer things are being created just around the corner. America is still new— a mere pup in nationhood building compared to the nations of the world. America is still warm and happily drooling like a little fat baby full of newness and the unanticipated consequences of its poo.

When the first public statement of the President of the United States after the 9/11 catastrophe was to "keep shopping," it was clear that faith in newness reigned supreme. Across the country, new properties always command higher prices than older properties, and new shopping malls snatch customers from the mom and pop stores that everyone loved.

New products are greeted with enthusiasm and discarded almost as fast because the next versions will always include improvements or new gadgets. The past "Thank God," is passed along with its mistakes and errors and lessons, and responsibilities. Why cling to the past when the future has given us the smartphone over the telegraph line, Sponge Bob over news shows, and coated aspirins over cold baths?

Dear Reader,

You will notice here that I'm not following my own good advice as mentioned above, *"Don't assume that because Americans speak English, they understand English the way an English person speaks it, or in fact how others use English."*

Because irony and sarcasm are in the mind of the beholder, and because, as mentioned earlier, Americans "don't care" for irony. But freedom wouldn't mean anything if one didn't exercise it, and for me, freedom means saying what I feel. So the message here is that it's important to exercise a freedom but to be aware that it sometimes comes with a cost. Or as the adage goes, "You have to pay the cost to be the boss."

Yours in truth and freedom - Ian

Choice and the illusion of it is as sacred to True Americans as newness and machine-made apple pies! Real Americans love to indulge their attitudes about choice. And they exercise it as much as possible, by disregarding a perfectly good product, service or essential piece of information just to see what the other "choice" offers.

That's why True Americans elect so many people: presidents, governors, judges, senators, congressmen, and dogcatchers. Real Americans never commit themselves to anything in life. Leaders who cannot be changed—like monarchs—make True Americana nervous.

Real Americans reserve the right to change decisions "whenever and whatever." Anything less is an attack on personal freedom and a reminder of what dictatorships must be like. Limited choice makes True Americans uneasy; they even get edgy when their favorite fruit is out of season. Nowhere do people view restrictions with more alarm than in America. For this reason, True Americans mistrust package holidays and long-term investments.

Contracts of employment must always contain appropriate "get out" clauses. Real Americans plan vacations and shop for Christmas at the last minute and make final decisions only after all possible choices have been considered. Real Americans love conducting business by phone because they're deadly afraid of committing anything to paper. The right to substitute a tossed salad for French fries is enshrined in the Constitution. To be a real American is to live life à la carte.

Choice is the same thing as freedom, which is the same thing as money, which is the same thing as being American, and that's the real secret of Real Americans' fondness for cash. It's not that Real Americans are by nature greedier or needier than the rest of the world. It's just that Real Americans admire money more openly. Real Americans see money as a measurement of individual worth and value and the final guarantee of personal choice.

Because, money is power—and power is a good thing! Lack of cash means you lack ability, which makes you a loser. Money is a hedge against being a loser. Plus, you can take it with you to your grave by forcing your kin to engrave your name on some building that people will have to pay to visit—or, if you've got enough, you may not have to go at all; cash gives you room to maneuver. If it turns out that death is optional—and science comes up with a miracle—your dollars guarantee that you won't be ignored. Money buys the best, and the best is the True American birthright.

Miss Piggy, from "Sesame Street," that great Real American, said it best: "Moi—I come first." When she performed her weekly show, she touched a chord deep in the hearts of her country-people. Real Americans consider their first duty and obligation to be to look after #1—themselves.

This follows the logic of "I'm going to live forever," and "good guys come last" because it stands to reason that, if you don't see yourself as being #1, then you're not going to last, and how will you face heaven knowing you didn't try as hard as you could to stay out of that place.

Therefore, each Real American must concentrate on attaining his or her "best personal attitude" and achieve supreme inner selfish fulfillment—which in an Ayn Rand philosophic world will create a society of better individuals, and by extension, a better world—because we will be the selfish-est nation in the world.

Real Americans don't have to read *The Wealth of Nations* because they intrinsically support and understand the great ideas of Adam Smith, the economist whose theory claimed that the individual working in his own self-interest leads ultimately to the highest good for all people and all countries. A strong society is merely the sum of strong individual parts. America is the heartland of individualism.

You protect your own interests by making choices—lots of them. If you acquire money—which gives you more leverage—then so much the better. For Real Americans the real national anthem is "I Did It My Way" by Frank Sinatra. Now, he was a True American.

To succeed in America, you must be "cute." This should be interpreted in its broadest sense like a metaphysical concept. It refers not just too selfish brats (children whose parents refuse to hold them accountable for bad behavior) but to being arresting, appealing, charismatic, and worthy of celebrity.

Specific abilities are not necessary—although they can be useful in framing you as a part of a group. Through money, contacts or prostituting yourself in some unique way, in public, you may vibrate at the same frequency as the American culture—the resonance of never-ending excitement! This is the true meaning of success.

Anyone, anything, and any idea can be called cute—so the term is lavishly applied. Newborn babies are cute, Doppler radar is cute, Denzel Washington is cute—and so are Star Wars technology, raspberry popcorn, some sit-coms, and selected restaurants. Even serious corporations can get "cute."

For instance, an astute American businesswoman called Meg decides to name her financial consultancy "Meg-a-bucks." "Cute" scratches a national itch. It describes everything you want someone (or something) to be. "Cute" is instant gratification, wish fulfillment. It has about it the delight of a fantasy come true. Presidents can be cute…and virtually must be video-cute to win.

President Obama is very, very cute and he knows it. He is a national turn-on: cute-looking, cute personality, and even cuter sense of humor. Remember how cute Obama was when he ran around the White House grounds chasing his dog? At times, it seems he can do no wrong. Congress hates that he's so cute. Many world leaders (including President Bush but not Senator Gore) have drawn essential lessons from this.

President Bush knew how to be cute (and little else). Nixon knew everything else but wasn't a bit cute. Bill Clinton can be cute when he puts his considerable mind to it. Donald Trump is not one of life's natural cuties; however, the charm bred of expressing totally bigoted lies repeatedly —is unstoppable. It works for the young and for the geriatric. And if you're cute enough, you can have virtually anything. America is up for grabs.

IN AMERICA—DON'T LOOK BACK

The good old times & places—are gone!
All times in the past appeared good!
Great things have been and yet might be
greater still If we humans had the will
to play our tricks in a wider field.

STEP FOUR - ESL (OR ENGLISH AS A STUPID LANGUAGE)

English has a major flaw; it was invented by English people! They stole words and phrases from every language in the world to distinguish themselves from most of the earth's population because they believe themselves to be God's chosen people—unfortunately, somebody else stole that idea before them!

The historic irony today is that English is the de-facto World language, and now English people witness every day the betrayal of their beloved class-based language bastardized by the people they conquered, as well as the rest of the world!

Because of England's early imperialist history, English is spoken around the globe and is as much a cultural assault on its colonized people as it is on their own lower classes. English is a hybrid language that borrowed freely from every language in the world with no thought to its fluency. English has created a dissonance between the way one speaks English and the way one writes the language.

Most languages can be understood across cultures because the spoken word is the same as, or like, the written word. English, rather devilishly, cannot be understood in this way. To speak and write English one is forced to undergo a cultural transformation that spits in the eye of effective communication.

To learn English is to be subjected to the equivalent of the rack, where the tools needed to speak the language are opposed to the tools needed to write English. As a result, nobody has any idea who William Shakespeare was and why he left us so few clues as to his brilliance and understanding of the language he made famous.

As an ESL teacher, I have never had a class of students whom all share the same learning styles. As a result, I have to teach my students first, how to learn before I teach them what to learn. There are many styles of learning.

The range of learning styles is expansive, beginning with the physical sense we have about learning, the way we interact with people and our style of thinking and absorbing information, along with cultural and historical factors.

Knowing that some students are more comfortable learning by rote, or through visual tools (flashcards, videos, drawings and maps and the like), or kinesthetic methods (through role-playing, simulations, and field trips), for example, makes it essential that I design my class programs to incorporate the appropriate learning styles that meet my students' needs.

Of course, people can change, but they need instruction. People need demonstrations of alternative learning styles that they can make their own.

In my classes, I include a variety of exercises to emphasize the previously mentioned styles, as well as debates, chain-stories, and word games to help strengthen my students' verbal skills; dictation, listening and dialog exercises to stimulate auditory skills; puzzles and problem solving to stimulate logical/analytical skills; and pair and group work to stimulate interpersonal skills.

Combining these and other learning styles is an essential ingredient of my teaching methods. If a student learns best through verbal and visual styles, and I present her/him with a program full of logical/analytical tasks, it created frustration for both of us because I'm not communicating effectively with that student.

Knowing the different kinds of learning styles and strategies is critical to teaching ESL and allows me to encourage all my students to learn in their way while also introducing them to additional ways by which they can learn.

As an ESL instructor who teaches Spanish, Arabic, Chinese, Vietnamese and French speakers, I'm always approached by people, who wonder why I don't speak all those languages. I explain to them that to learn a language, you must first hear it, which requires learning to listen. Simultaneously, you must speak what you hear, and practice daily what you hear. By accumulating new words daily, you build vocabulary.

LEARN FIRST HOW TO LEARN; THEN LEARN ENGLISH

"The only man who is educated is the man who has learned how to learn; the man who has learned how to adapt and change; the man who has realized that no knowledge is secure, that only the process of seeking knowledge gives a basis for security." ~ Carl Rogers (1969)

Learning a foreign language is not rocket science. It's all based on how well you know yourself and how well you can use all your capacities to practice the new sounds and words you hear.

If you want to learn English—and motivation is eighty percent of your success—you need strategies. What follows are some strategies for you, so read them one by one carefully and think about how you can use each of them in your unique learning process.

1. *BEGIN:*
- Open your mind and be sure of the goals you want to achieve by learning this language. Write down your ideas and reasons for learning!
- Do you want to learn English because you want to get an English-speaking girlfriend or boyfriend? Alternatively, is it because some members of your family speak English and you want to understand them?
- Are you aiming to get a promotion or a specific position in your company?
- Do you want to learn English because you like the sound of the language?
- Do you need to fill your free time by learning something?

2. *JUST WRITE IT DOWN!*
- Every time you feel despair in your learning process, write it down, along with the reasons. Create a list of reasons that help you understand the difficulties and allow you to set your goals and avoid getting distracted!

3. *SELECT A SPECIFIC TIME FOR YOUR LEARNING.*
- In your daily routine, take 20 minutes, 30 minutes, an hour each day, whatever time is available to you for your learning. You must make sure that learning English is as important to you as eating, socializing, taking a shower, having a coffee or tea, or the myriad of other things that you make time for in your day.
- Switch between mornings, afternoons and evenings on different days because, depending on your daily routine, you'll feel different, so your feelings and receptiveness to learning is different.

4. *Choose only one or two language items at a time.*
- Don't be greedy. Remember that learning English is a process. Also, don't treat your memory as if it were a computer hard disc. We are humans, and our memory is limited.
- When you learn a item, **feel it** (in other words, imagine situations in which you can use the words or expressions you are learning).

5. *Learn the basics—select what you want to learn first*
- When you are planning how to learn English, you must prioritize.
- Imagine the circumstances in which you use these new words and phrases you're learning: Are you going to a party where there are many English-speaking people? Then, introductions and greetings are your main priority. Alternatively, if you are going to be traveling around an English-speaking country, you want to concentrate on learning phrases that help you buy a ticket or ask for information.

REMEMBER TO LEARN THE BASICS FIRST!

6. *Practice what you are learning during intervals of repetition.*
- When you are learning a new word, you must repeat it a few times first, and after a short interval, recall it again. Choose intervals between five seconds and a minute.

NOTHING BEATS A FAILURE BUT A TRY.

7. *ASSESS YOURSELF ALL THE TIME.*
- Learn words and expressions in both languages (English and your native language) and recall the English word or expression in your language and vice-versa.

8. *PUT WORDS TOGETHER; THEN INCREASE YOUR TALKING SPEED.* Try to remember how fast you'd say the same thing in your mother tongue and say it at the same speed in English. Run the words together with the way an English native speaker would.

9. *BALANCE YOUR LEARNING WITH READING, WRITING, LISTENING AND SPEAKING SKILLS.*
- However, every time you say, write, read or listen to something, feel it!

10. *WHEN SPEAKING THE LANGUAGE, GUESS!*
- Remember that guessing is about twenty-five percent of the secret of how to learn English and how to speak it. Don't feel embarrassed because you understood or said something wrong. Say "sorry" and carry on.
- Good learners of English are willing to guess.

11. *MAKE AN EFFORT TO COMMUNICATE AND DON'T BE SHY.*
- Good students of English have a strong drive to communicate or to learn from communications. They are serious about how to learn English, so they are willing to do many things to get their message across.

12. *DON'T BE AFRAID TO MAKE MISTAKES!*
- Good learners of English want to communicate. They are willing to live with a certain amount of vagueness. They are often willing to appear foolish.

13. Learn the language rules and patterns.
- In addition to focusing on communication, good students of English are prepared and continually looking for patterns and rhythms in the language. For instance, in how many every-day situations can you use the question "Can I have?" [kan-eye-hav]?
- Sound out the words (in your language if necessary).
- Get used to making a connection to how the sound is written

14. Good learners of English practice.
   Practice makes perfect.

15. Good learners of English are always looking to improve.
- Good learners are continually attending to how well their speech is received and whether their performance meets the standards they have set themselves.

16. Good learners of English learn about how the language works.
- It is essential to pay attention to the grammar of the language, how it is used, as well as the body language and tone of voice of the one speaking.

17. Good learners of English speak in English every time they have an opportunity to do so.
- Many times, you'll have the choice of speaking in English or your native language, but when the people you are speaking too also speak both languages, don't hesitate to speak English all the time!

STEP FIVE – ONLY IN AMERICA
(based on the poem 'The Incident' by Countee Cullen)

Standing in a compound in Accra, Ghana, Irene said goodbye to her 16-year-old son Kofi.

"Now, Kofi, I want you to be very careful of who you talk to. Your father has arranged for a chauffeur to pick you up at the airport in San Francisco. Stay with him always, and don't wander off, like I know you like to do. Do you understand?"

"Yes, Mommy."

"And don't forget to visit with your auntie in Oakland and your cousins in Antioch. And before I forget, take this bottle of palm wine to your uncle. Your daddy will know where he is staying now."

"But, Mommy, I don't think they will let me bring drinks into America."

"O, don't be silly; it's only a little palm wine. Now…" She grabbed his shoulders, straightened his stance. She touched his tie and tried to smile as tears welled up in her eyes. The house steward began placing Kofi's two bags in the back of the family Mercedes. The mother turned her head away from Kofi, with one hand covering her face, the other still holding onto her son. Kofi tried to avoid crying too. They both struggled with their feelings of separation.

"You'd better go now so that Clarence can get you to the airport on time." She said through tears, "Be careful, my son;

God willing you will come home safe." She spun around and scurried into the house.

"Yes, Mommy. I will. Bye." Kofi was momentarily paralyzed. His emotions held him to the spot, yet his will was bursting to embrace his new adventure.

"Mr. Kofi," said Clarence, the house steward, and driver, "we need to get going now if we're to get to the airport in time." Kofi moved towards the car, wiping his eyes, sticking out his chest, and took a last look back at his home. He saw his mother and younger sisters crowding around the window waving to him. He waved back and stepped into the car. Clarence gunned the Mercedes, and they leave a trail of dust on the half-tarmacked roadway as they sped down the road.

Kofi arrived at San Francisco Airport, wearing an Afro batik shirt and beige slacks and carrying a big brown paper bag. He exited the customs hall into the middle of a throng of people looking through him for their own friends and family members; he was soon carried along by the human current out into the terminal waiting area.

Kofi was so excited at finally getting off the long flight from Ghana, West Africa and arriving safely, he had a bright smile on his face as he craned his neck to look for the driver who he was told would be waiting for him. He saw a big African-American man in a cap and uniform with a sign that read: MR. KOFI ACHEMPONG. Kofi approached the chauffeur.

"Mr. Cof-fee Ach-eM-pung?" said the man.

"Yes, that's me," said Kofi bemused at the strange pronunciation of his name.

"Your father sent me to pick you up," said the man. "We'll meet him at the house. Do you have any bags?"

"Yes."

"On which baggage carousel did they say they would be on?"

"On number four, I think."

"Come this way, please." Kofi walked hurriedly next to the big chauffeur, looking up at him and catching his attempts at smiles while he looked down at Kofi who smiled nervously under the shadow of this huge man. The chauffeur leads Kofi to a limo outside the airport terminal building as the chauffeur moved around to the back door and opened it for Kofi to get in. He helped him into the limo and closed the door before going to the rear of the limo, paying off the airport attendant who had put Kofi's bags in the trunk; then he moved around to the driver's side and got in.

The chauffeur started the engine, which purrs into life, then pulled smoothly away from the curb and into the flow of traffic leaving the airport terminal. Riding along the freeway towards San Francisco, Kofi saw huge billboards and flashing signs that were many stories high, beautifully painted and filled with photographs. Each image took in Kofi's full attention as the colors, designs, and vividness of the curvaceous figures of the women on the billboards stimulate complicated sensuous feelings in him. But they flash by so quickly that he barely has time to consider what they mean, let alone what they were selling. He had not learned the visual cultural language of American public advertising yet.

"You from Africa, aren't you?" said the chauffeur, "I know it soon as I saw you. I can tell an' African nigger from an' American nigger any day. You guys are kind of shy and have that deep droning way of talking." He talked into his windscreen watching the road looking back occasionally at Kofi whose face was pressed against the side window as he tried to take in the dazzling city images flashing by through the smoky glass.

"Do they teach you to speak English with that weird accent, or does it come out like that 'cause of your African language?" The chauffeur turned to Kofi to punctuate his question. Kofi, only half listening, remembered his manners and responded absentmindedly.

"O, yes, we all learn to speak English with the same accent."

The chauffeur nodded his head, reassured that he was right all along about Africans. "I've never been to Africa meself, but a buddy of mine says he knows a guy who went to Guyana, and it was so poor he had to stay at the Hilton hotel. The first time he'd ever been in a Hilton anywhere. Niggers ain't allowed in no Hilton in these United Snakes, least not to stay; maybe to work in the laundry, hahaha!"

While the chauffeur talked, Kofi explored the inside of the limo. He tried to answer politely when the chauffeur directed questions at him, but the chauffeur continued his monologue without requiring a response. It was as if the closeness to a person from Africa had evoked in the chauffeur an inquiry within himself to test what African-ness he had or did not have. Kofi's eyes bulged out at the phone, mini TV, and the drinks cabinet that mechanically materializes from the back of the chauffeur's seat, with the touch of a button. "Just here for the holidays, then?" the chauffeur asked directly.

"Yes," Kofi nodded and tried to say something, but the chauffeur cut him off and continued talking.

"Well, you've come to the greatest country in the world, Coffee." he said, "Only in America can you see all the peoples of the world living together in one place. We got everybody here: blacks, whites, yellows, and red peoples. We got men who wanna be women and women who wanna be men! Yeah, we got everybody, and everybody wants to come to America 'cause we got it all, and we've got the best shit here, which they could never git away with back home!"

The chauffeur talked over his shoulder at Kofi and occasionally turned around to face Kofi, to emphasize a point and to see if he's was taking in all this great wisdom. "I read a story the other day that these here Viet-mees rowed across the Pacific just to git to America. Now that's some determination, and it goes to show you just how much peoples wanna come here. And we niggers don't do too bad either. Sure, the white man's gonna keep all the big shit for himself; I'd do the same if I were in his position, but we gits our chances."

Kofi looked out at the Pyramid building as they approached downtown San Francisco on highway I-80 heading towards the Bay Bridge and the East Bay. The chauffeur began another monologue as Kofi pretended to listen while eating up the visual candy tapestry moving in front of his eyes.

"Of course, some of them niggers at Hunter's Point are always complainin', no matter what the white man does for 'em. Just look at me. I used to work in an airplane factory in LA. I come up from Arkansas wid my folks, but they were old and died soon after. So, I worked that stinking job for eight years, 'til a buddy of mine brings me up here promising to help me get a catering job – I use to do some cooking back in Arkansas. Okay, so it was only bar-b-q pits for black folks!

Peoples loved my sauces, and everyone says I should be a chef – anyways, there was no job. That's when I ran into your dad. We struck up a conversation at a Giants game; that's baseball; you hip to baseball? Do they have baseball in Africa – of course, they don't. Well never mind! Your dad stepped out of the VIP lounge and bumped into me coming back from the hot dog stand. Well, he knocked my hot dog, ketchup, and soda all over my shirt and pants.

I was mad at myself 'cause I was rushing back to my seat after the seventh-inning stretch. Well, he bought me another hot dog, gave me some money to dry-clean my clothes, and before long we were like friends. He kept asking me all kinds of questions about baseball, which I was happy to share 'cause I use to be a player back in the day. He asked me what I do, and I said I was looking for work. He gave me his card, shook my hand and goes back to his VIPs. A week later I gits a call from this white woman, saying Mr. Ach-eM-pung would like to offer me a job as his personal chauffeur. And here I is; your daddy's one hell of a guy! Hold on there; I gotta stop here briefly, Cof-fee. Just hang loose."

The limo pulled up to a café in The Mission district. Kofi could see lots of paintings on the sides of houses and a big scroll that reads "The Mission." The chauffeur approached a group of Latino kids. Kofi found the button to lower the window and listened to the chauffeur talking with his friends.

"Hey, Amigo, my nigger, 'what 'appen'?"

"Hey, Jose, Que pasa'. You my nigger, man! What you got fo' me?"

The chauffeur stepped into the shadow of the café, and Kofi could see that he was putting something in his pocket. Kofi lost interest in their activities and looked up and down the street at the colorful murals adorning the sides of buildings. Groups of men in large cowboy hats, and matching embroidered shirts and pants, carry guitars of different sizes, move in and out of shop doorways.

A woman in a floral dress carrying baskets of flowers approached Kofi holding the stems of bright flowers up to Kofi's face. Kofi breathed in the spicy odor of a roadside taco stand and watched with envy a man bending his head underneath his raised hand, struggling to catch the sauce of his burrito that was dripping into his mouth as he walked away from the stand almost bumping into a light pole.

The chauffeur winked at Kofi as he got back into the limo, and said, "I got to make a stop in China Town and on California Street. Then it's home. O.K.?"

Kofi settled back into the thick leather seat of the limo and wallowed in the thrill of luxury that surrounded him. He had never been in such luxury before, and he was determined to enjoy every minute of it. The car moved off down Mission Street the kaleidoscope of murals and Latino-titled shop-fronts lined the street where groups of men and women, using exaggerated gestures of their hands and arms, filled the air with their laughter.

Under the freeway, Kofi was in awe of the massive concrete structures that blotted out the sky. The numerous factory-like buildings that bordered the highway have bright colors and shapes exaggeratedly large that engulfed the windows of the many storied high buildings. As they approached downtown San Francisco, the buildings crowd out the sun. Soon, the canyons of concrete and glass flooded their stretch limo in shadows as if it was perpetual night in that part of the city.

The chauffeur crossed Market Street at 5th and began weaving up and down and around pedestrian-packed sidewalks. As they streaked a path up Grant Street between the parked cars, ambling tourists, and crisscross traffic of hawkers and sellers flooding the street. The exotic oriental art and designs bursting out of the shop fronts onto the sidewalks held Kofi spellbound. The chauffeur pulled up to a pagoda-tiled structure. Two middle-aged Chinese men approached the car with a large package wrapped in brown paper.

"Hey, John Chew, how you doing? You got the old man's laundry?"

"Yes, Mister Man. You take good care; this special order. How you do? Mister Nigger Man? You look cool, Brother Man. You come back after work; have some good chow mein for you."

"Hey, man, watch with that nigger shit!" The chauffeur said with a serious scowl on his face. "Any other nigger hears you talk like that, but I would kick your butt!" He smiled at the panic that suddenly covered John Chew's face. "But don't worry; I won't tell. You sure is my nigger, Ha, Ha, Ha." As they pulled away from the curb, the chauffeur passed the bundle back to Kofi, who could see that it was a collection of pressed shirts. "That guy, John Chew, he cracks me up." said the chauffeur, "He's always trying to be Black. But every time he says 'Nigger,' I swear I want to roll him like some cracker barrel! Well, let's get you home now.

When they arrived at his father's house, Kofi was met at the front door by an excited woman. "Welcome to America Coffee," said Joyce, Kofi's father American wife. "Is that how I should say your name?" Her arms were outstretched and on her face was a warm, welcoming smile. But Kofi just looked at her forced a smile and extended his right hand. Quickly adjusting, Joyce's smiled faded to slight embarrassment as she took Kofi's hand in both of hers and directed him into the house. "Your father will be along soon. He's at the office." She leads Kofi into the house, where he is sucked into a sea of people. Hands and arms reach out to hug him, shake his hand and slap him on the back; everyone is excitedly welcoming him into the family.

After the introductions, which whirled around Kofi like a merry-go-ride, Kofi was taken aside by everyone in turn and told the secret of their success dramatically. The gathering was full of affluent African-Americans. Kofi wandered into the kitchen and arrived just in time to hear the following story, among three men, fashionably dressed and with glasses of beer in their hands.

"Niggers can really lie too, man," said Mike, "Did you hear the one about the two niggers who wanted to find out who had the biggest dick? Well, they didn't want to do it in public. They may have been dumb niggers, but they weren't freaks (laughs). So, they went to the Golden Gate Bridge and seeing all that water, they both decided to take a leak. Then one nigger says to the other, "Man, the water sure is cold," and the other nigger says, "and deep too!" The three bursts out laughing. (*** "Mud bone" See Richard Pryor).

Cherry overheard her husband Mike and his friends laughing loudly, a look of embarrassed irritation came over her face as she noticed Kofi standing behind Mike listening and confused at what he was hearing. She pulled Mike to the side, "Mike, you should be ashamed of yourself. What if the kid overheard you? You'll give him the impression niggers (she says this low under her breath, looking around the room) are all crazy."

Mike was still laughing and briefly tried to show a contrite face but soon turned back to his two drinking buddies unabashed as they continued to laugh, holding their hands over their mouths. Kofi moved to the kitchen table where he helped himself to some chicken and potato salad. As he walked through to the living room, he found a seat on the sofa next to a woman with an explosion of hair that seems to be held in place by a tiger striped ribbon that matched her tight tiger skin dress.

Her legs were exposed by slits up the side of each leg to her waist; the dress material covered her front. She was radiating a thick musty perfume that filled the atmosphere around her. She had her back to Kofi and was talking to a similarly dressed woman whose fingernails were two inches long and curved like those of an unkempt cat.

"Oh, I just love plastic, Girl!" said Gina, the woman in the tight skin dress. "I love to lay those cute cards out and fondle them every night before I go to bed. MasterCard is my love and happiness. Niggers don't understand that the way to a woman's heart is not through sweet talking jive, Honey, but through an American Express card."

Kofi overheard another conversation, across the room, as he tried to focus on his food.

"No, man," said Tony, "You ain't getting me saying the N-word, uh huh. No way! I can still feel the sting of my mama's hand on my face when she heard me saying it. And that was nearly twenty years ago."

Kofi got up from the sofa and walked around looking at the adults partying; he was the only kid there. He caught the end of a statement by a young man in dreads, who was maybe five years older than him, talking to some adults who were trying to distance themselves from the young man.

"...everyone uses the word 'nigger' now," said Rashid. "Just when we thought the word was outlawed, along comes Chris Rock and his ugly crew to make it fashionable again. You'll notice that Chris Rock uses it as a put-down of the Black underclass. He uses it in front of his audience of Black middle-class professionals who want to feel superior to the Black underclass.

That is until they get stopped by the police. Then, suddenly, niggers are their brothers! It was bad enough when just Blacks were using it; now every cracker under the sun is using it. It's just cultural currency now, for being down with the brothers and sisters..."

As the afternoon dissolved into the evening, most of the party guests went home, and Kofi found himself feeling tired from jet lag and he soon fell asleep on one of the sofas. Suddenly he awakened by a sharp tug, and when he opened his eyes, there was his stepmother, Joyce, staring down at him with a big smile.

"Your father's here," she said. Kofi leaped up found his way to his father's office and walked into the room where his father was hunched over his desk.

"Hi, Daddy!" said Kofi, excitement shining through his bleary eyes. His father looked up from his desk with slight annoyance but then broke into a big smile as he recognizes his son. He stopped writing, took off his glasses and stood up to receive his son coming around the desk to give him a big hug.

"It's great to see you, son! How have you been? Sorry, I wasn't at the airport, but I'm up to my neck in work just now, got to keep those bills paid. I hope your flight was okay? How'd you like riding in that limo?"

"It was great, Dad. I've never been in a car that big before."

"How's your mother? Did she receive my last check?"

"She's okay. She told me to thank you by God's grace, for all the help you're giving the family back in Ghana."

"So, how's the new house construction coming along? And what about Uncle Gordon and your Grandma?"

"They're all doing well by God's grace. We've just got to do the plumbing now for the house."

"How long will you stay this time?"

"I have to go back to school in a week. I have a big exam to take for a scholarship for Legion University, the most important university in Ghana. Mommy wants me to get this so bad."

"It's good that you've got ambition, son. One day, when you've got your degree, maybe you can come and work with me here in America. Would you like that?"

"Yes, I think so, although my Uncle Charles wants me to help him with his construction business in Accra."

"Well, it's good you have options. Anyway, while you're here, make sure you get to spend some time in San Francisco." Father and son hugged each other again. Soon after Kofi left the room so that his father could get back to work.

The next day Kofi's was back inside the limo looking out onto the streets of San Francisco as the chauffer took Kofi on a trip around the city. Kofi saw all the tourist sites – Pier 39, Ghirardelli Square, Market Street, the hotels and theaters, at Union Square, the restaurants and bars in North Beach, and on, and on…

The chauffeur took Kofi to Payless, Long's and Albertson's to buy toiletries and gifts that Kofi could take back to Ghana, where such things are in short supply. Kofi and the chauffeur were soon loaded down with bags and boxes that surround Kofi in the back of the limo.

While looking in Macy's window in Union Square, Kofi saw the reflection of a white boy staring at him. The boy was about the same age as Kofi. Kofi turned around and smiled at him. The white boy made an ugly grimace with his face as if imitating a monkey, then yelled out: "Nigger!" Kofi was startled and pained and looked at his own face in the reflected mirror to try and see how this white boy could make such a terrible mistake – Kofi didn't look anything like a monkey. The chauffeur didn't see the incident, and Kofi returned to the limo sad and deeply irritated by the uncalled-for behavior.

A week later Kofi flew back to Ghana and was met by Clarence, the family steward, who drove him back to his home in the family Mercedes. When they arrived at the house, Kofi somberly approached his mother.

"So how was your trip, my son? How was your great adventure to A-mer-i-ca, and the sights of San-Fran-sis-co?"

"It was interesting, Mommy." he said with a quizzical look, "but everywhere I went, people kept using this word 'nigger'! What does 'nigger' mean, Mommy?". His mother, her hand suddenly when to her throat as she stood in shock and pained incomprehension. She pulled her son to her and buried his head in her breasts, crying softly; to herself

"Oh, it's nothing. It doesn't mean anything. Don't let it worry you." Still, Kofi couldn't help feeling that of all the things he'd experienced on his trip to America nothing hurt him as much as being called a nigger.

STEP SIX – THE ART OF COMMUNICATING

An essential part of learning a language is speaking. Most of us don't practice speaking, even in our own language. We do plenty of talking and growling and shouting and complaining, but we don't speak with the idea that we want the listener to hear and understand what we are saying.

Communication requires an intention to make clear what you have to say. As the communicator, you are one hundred percent responsible for being understood. The listener is not obliged to figure out what you meant to say. In everyday conversation, when we visually interact with someone, we have the benefit of watching that person's body language responding to our words.

Body language represents some fifty-five percent of the information communicated to us by someone we're talking to. The tone with which they speak provides another thirty-eight percent of the information we use to make a judgment about a person, and only seven percent of their verbal language registers as important to us. We can see the results of this from the political classes, who make some of the stupidest statements. Yet they're always well dressed and coiffed, and their tone is still soothing and patronizing.

The effectiveness of communication has more to do with the appropriate presentation than it does with authenticity. Therefore, most people have difficulty with public speaking—they get confused between what they say and how to say it.

The political class has no problem with this contradiction—they always babble first and worry about meaning second! However, if you or I really want to communicate sincerely, we must control the articulation of our voice and our physical presentation, which can be improved with a few simple exercises. With some focused attention, we can project to another person the image, attitude, and sound we want him or her to hear.

Learning a language is like being an actor auditioning for a part. The part you are going for is the role of a fluent English speaker. To improve voice dexterity—exercising the muscles we use to talk—there are several exercises available. Each person needs to explore and find those that work best for him or her. I include some here as part of a five-minute warm-up exercise program for improving speech:

LIP EXERCISES:

a) Sit upright and purse your lips together. Lift the pursed lips toward your nose, as far as possible, and keep them there for a count of 5; repeat 5 times.
b) Pucker your lips slightly and try to bring the corners of your mouth together. Hold for a count of 5; repeat 5 times.
c) Keeping your lips and teeth together, smile as broadly as possible without opening your lips. Hold for a count of 5; repeat 5 times.
d) Pucker your lips in a kiss. Keep and hold for a count of 5; repeat 5 times.
e) With your puckered lips closed, curl them in toward your mouth across your teeth. Hold for a count of 5; repeat 5 times.

CHEEK EXERCISES:
a) Pucker and pout your lips using your cheek muscles. Hold for a count of 5; repeat 5 times.
b) With your lips closed, smile a relaxed smile and then suck your cheek muscles towards your eyes for a count of 5; repeat 5 times.
c) Pucker your top lip. Turn the corners of your lips upward and move your cheek muscles towards your eyes for a count of 5; repeat 5 times.
d) Smile as widely as possible (with lips and teeth closed); try to get the corners of your mouth to touch your ears, for a count of 5; repeat 5 times.

WARM-UP EXERCISES BEFORE A SPEECH:

1) PREPARATION:
- Feet apart, stretch up tall.
- Bend from the waist, releasing one vertebra at a time.
- Knees bent, try touching your fingers to the floor.
- Raise your trunk slowly, vertebra by vertebra, making an "HA" sound on every out breath.
- Stand erect and swing your arms in large circles, one arm at a time.
- Say "HA, HAHA, HAHA" as you warm up your throat. Repeat the following sounds, back to front:

VOICELESS	VOICED
(sharp/one sound)	(resonant/vibrating sound)
K – KA	G – GA (back of your throat)
T – TA	D – DA
L – LA	N – NA
P – PA	B – BA
F – FA	M – MA
V – VA (at the front of your mouth)	

2) *Relaxation:*
   - Yawn, and inhale deeply.
   - Stretch your jaw as wide open as possible.
   - Vocalize as you exhale, "Aaaaaah!"

3) *Breath Control:*
   - Breathe in deeply and fully.
   - Exhale as slowly as possible through rounded lips.

4) *Humming:*
   - Starting at a low pitch that is easy for you:
     o Hum one octave up the scale slowly:
       DO—RAY—ME—FA—SO—LA—TEE—DO
   - Hum four prolonged "M's" on each breath.

5) *Singing:*
   - Sing with wide open mouth the
   - DO—ME—SO—DO—SOL—ME—DO tune.
     (C   E   G   C   G   E   C)
   - Vary the exercise using MOH, MAW, MEE, MAH.

6) *Intoning:*
   - Repeat the above exercise but keep the speech pitch at or near a singing tone.

7) *Resonating:*
   - Say the following phrases loudly, one to breathe, lengthening the vowels:

     D-o-wn and O-u-t, N-o-w and Th-e-n, Wh-o A-r-e Y-o-u, M-e and M-i-n-e-,
     F-a-r A-w-a-y, H-e-r-e To-d-a-y, A-ro-u-nd To-n-e,
     H-o-ld Y-o-u-r V-o-w-e-ls

8) *ARTICULATING:*
- Say the following limerick or any that you know by heart, in less than 10 seconds. Keep the consonants sharp:

    A Tutor who tooted the flute
    Tried to tutor two tutors to toot.
    Said the two tutors to the Tutor
    Is it harder to toot, or
    Tutor two tutors to toot?

9) *PROJECTING:*
- Recite the following poem in a full slow voice with lengthened vowels, lengthened M's, N's and NG's, and with a well-opened mouth:

    Robert Browning's "Meeting at Night"

    The grey sea and the long black land;
    And the yellow half-moon large and low;
    And the startled little waves that leap
    In fiery ringlets from their sleep,
    As I gain the cove with pushing prow,
    And quench its speed, i' the slushy sand.

    Then a mile of warm sea-scented beach;
    Three fields to cross till a farm appears;
    A tap at the pane, the quick sharp scratch
    And blue spurt of lighted match,
    And a voice less loud, thro' its joys and fears,
    Than the two hearts beating each to each!

10) *INTERPRETING (REPEAT TO YOURSELF):*
- I inhale strongly just before I read each line.
- I speak the line easily, without strain.
- I exhale through my mouth as I read aloud.

- I do not try to control the outflow of my breath.
- I give conscious attention to breathing in only.
- I inhale either after each line or at the end of two lines.

11) USING TONGUE TWISTERS (REPEAT TO YOURSELF):
- I Saw Susie sitting in a shoe shine shop. Where she sits she shines, and where she shines she sits.

- The thirty-three thieves thought that they thrilled the throne throughout Thursday.

- Picky people pick Peter Pan peanut butter; it's the peanut butter picky people pick.

- Around the rugged rocks the ragged rascal ran.

- Betty better butter Brad's bread better!

- If Stu chews shoes, should Stu choose the shoes he chews?

IF YOU MAKE A DAILY HABIT OF THIS FIVE-MINUTE PROGRAM, YOU WILL SEE IMMEDIATE IMPROVEMENTS IN YOUR VOICE CONTROL AND PROJECTION WITHIN A WEEK.

HEART SONG

It's not with eyes of tears that I greet the
season's dawning. Nor do I chase like a
butterfly the threads of half-forgotten
tapestries. I sing no song of pain to raise
my muse, for she calls me in every mood,
a spirit fixed to my inner soul
—I have only to listen.

STEP SEVEN – GETTING A JOB

The last piece of the puzzle of coming to America is to find a job. Many immigrants continue to work within their own community, here in America and are thus subject to many of the same restrictions that held them down when they were in their home country. America, notwithstanding its particular historical prejudices, is a country that encourages everyone to open a shop and announce to the world that he or she is in business.

But to really take advantage of America, it's necessary to work effectively with Americans and learn the cultural language of the market-place. Americans love to spend money—unlike many Europeans (and I'm not pointing specifically at the British), but Americans require that you understand their consumer habits.

At some point, the new-comer, as well as people born here in America, needs to sharpen the skills required for job seeking and finding new career opportunities through job search/career development workshops. Based on my own experiences looking for and applying for work in America, I've created a program detailing what I've learned what to do and what not to do. Most importantly, I believe that if you can identify and focus on your key goals, you will find success, whatever the current job market may be.

In my personal interactive class, you will experience and participate in several exercises and discussions and assessments to explore your future job/career path. Participants will examine their motivations, skills, interests, values and work preferences to learn how to put them into action. This hands-on program will empower YOU!

In my Job Success workbook, participants are required to answer questions, list ideas, develop vocabulary, research information, write about their work experiences honestly, and identify their passions and goals. Research has shown that people learn best when they act out, write about, and talk about their ideas in groups. By making a personal commitment to their beliefs, they, in turn, own their thoughts and therefore their future.

Engagement with the material in my workbook, through writing, reading and discussion, is the workbook's purpose and therefore requires all participants to bring their focused attention and commitment to its study.

My program covers four (4) key areas over six (6) two- (2-) hour classes, which can be taken online or in a live workshop setting. The program includes:

1) A self-assessment test, which will help you identify your ideal job
2) Worksheets to help you develop your resume and cover letter
3) Public speaking and elevator speeches that will build your confidence in your interviewing skills
4) A "how-to" on developing your own job success strategy through understanding how the job market works and identifying and pursuing the job success you want

This workbook came out of my own experiences looking for work across different cultures, countries, industries, and careers over the past forty years, in both public and private enterprises.

I am originally from London, England, and as a young man of color coming of age in a profoundly color- and class-conscious environment, I learned quickly that, if I were to find employment, I needed to learn the rules of the society I was in. I had no time to dwell on the unfairness of the systems in which I was attempting to make my way. Irrational behavior by people in positions of power is a fact of life. The sooner you learn to focus on your goals and to acquire and exercise the skills and attitudes needed to survive in the world, the sooner you will be successful at living the life you want.

This workbook, then, is not from the perspective of a career counselor who studied how to help people in an MBA course; nor is it from the perspective of a career bureaucrat who manages the problematic programs of processing people in and out of the workforce. This workbook is written by a worker who continues to search for the perfect job.

I've worked in the oil industry in Scotland, as a Civil Engineer in London, a cook in Spain, a travel writer in France, Greece and Algeria, a teacher in Ghana, a Sales Executive in Sierra Leone and on a Kibbutz in Israel. I've been an owner of several businesses, including antiques, music distribution, radio, cable TV production, free-lance construction inspection, video documentaries, and I have been the president of a video poetry festival. I know what it takes to get a business up and running and keep it going. I understand the challenges and disappointments that every entrepreneur must face. I've worked for government and corporations, and I know the focus needed to succeed.

Along the way, I've written and published eight books, non-fiction books about culture and music, a book of short stories, one novel and books of poetry, and I continue to write and publish to this day. I think of myself as a poet who loves to teach the English language. I'm passionate about sharing my experiences with my students and learning about their experiences. I'm focused on the work of facing the challenge of the twenty-first century.

The worksheets in this manual are essential for you to complete. Through them, you will gain the confidence, focus, and persistence that will build positive habits you must have to get the job you want. You are not owed a job. Some people find this in conflict with American values. For those who believe there is a conflict here, I refer them to the history books.

The past is not about what should have been, but what happened. The present is all that you have in your hands to make your future. If you apply yourself to the exercises in my workbook, you will prove to yourself that you hold your job success in your own hands, and you deserve the job you want.

CULTURAL SIGNALS IN THE WORKPLACE

Stereotypes are understandably questionable ways to define people; however, it is a curious fact that most people spend half their time defining themselves by their own stereotypes and the rest of their time resenting being stereotyped by others!

With this caveat of acknowledgment that individuals are not stereotypes, please review the five corporate cultural styles presented below. These first-level categories are by their nature very general. Most corporations are combinations of all five styles in varying degrees. They are given here to make people aware of such customs and encourage people to research carefully the cultural environment they are going into when they apply for work.

1) Family: Status is ascribed to parent figures who are close and powerful.

2) Pyramid: Status is ascribed to superior roles who are distant yet powerful.

3) Project: Status is achieved by project group members who contribute to a targeted goal.

4) Start-Up: Status is achieved by individuals exemplifying creativity and growth.

5) Government: Status is achieved by position on the organizational chart.

After you understand a little about the five main cultural types that describe most corporate entities, you might also find it helpful to see some of how these cultural types play out in an organization.

Rules versus Relationships:
- The rules or universal cultural approach can be summed up this way: "What's good and right can be defined and is always apples." The "always apples" definition is a linear one that dictates exactly what is right or wrong.
- What is essential in relationship cultures is that friendship has special obligations and should come first. These cultures are more organic and less concerned with abstract social codes.

Groups versus Individuals:
- In group cultures, people consider themselves primarily as a part of the whole and believe that the community should come first.
- The individualist cultural approach believes that individualism is most important, and that individuals should be allowed to develop and contribute to the community as and when they wish.

Neutral versus Passionate:
- Neutrals believe that the nature of people's interactions should be objective and detached. The belief that it's "just business" or to be "cool." A primary assumption of this attitude is that people should resemble machines to operate businesses more efficiently.

Passionate cultures consider business a human affair where the whole gamut of emotions is seen as appropriate. Loud laughter, many people talking at the same time about different things in a meeting or leaving the conference room in anger during negotiation are all part of the business.

OPEN VERSUS SPECIFIC:
- In public business culture, the whole person is involved in a business relationship. There is real personal contact that may include integrating relationships inside and outside of business, such as family contacts.
- In specific business cultures, the business relationship is defined by written contracts, which set legal responsibilities for both parties before, during and at the end of that relationship.

ACHIEVEMENT VERSUS CONNECTIONS:
- Achievement cultures reward and admire people and groups based on what they have recently accomplished.
- Connection cultures reward people and groups based on their attributes of class, birth, school, colleges, kinship, and age.

When I was recommended to teach ESL (English as a Second Language) at a Spanish community center in the San Francisco Bay Area, I was excited at the prospect of both teaching English and learning to speak Spanish. I studied Spanish off and on for years after taking a trip to Cuba in the '90s and was fascinated by the culture and language, as well as the political resilience of the people.

However, even though my classes were well received by the adult students, I ran afoul of management—in fact, the white male manager. Although not a Spanish native, he had spent time in Central America where he'd learned the language and, more crucially, the culture of Latino business—Patriarchal/Family leadership. This type of business leadership applies to many countries and communities around the world.

Let me acknowledge that I know this is a stereotype, but as I've argued previously, most people of the world identify themselves by stereotypical behavior—although they don't like people outside of their group identifying them as such—so I would be remiss not to recognize people for how they are seen by others to behave.

Patriarchal/Family business structures are dominated by a single person, usually a man, but in many cultures, a woman. The exercise of power is paternal, the emotional and practical functions of control being held in one person's hands alone. These businesses are not run as businesses in the sense that they use every piece of reasoned information to maximize the human resources and profits of their company. No. The object of such a company is to maximize the power and control of the leader. This means no activity can go on without the okay of the boss directly.

We have multiple examples of this in America, as well as around the world. The Mafia runs its business this way; so do most Fortune 500 companies. However, in my experience with the Latino model, the Patriarch will absolutely refuse to exhibit any appearance of shared authority with another male.

The American version of the Patriarch is to extend limited—feel-good—roles of power to women, while controlling the most essential reins themselves. Of course, this model reflects the universal Patriarchal model that dominates our world, summed up by the "the celebrity," "the genius," and "the God-given-talented entertainer or sports person" through whom we live vicariously because of some messianic neurosis.

I encountered the Pyramid business structure in both England and America. This culture is defined by a series of increasingly superior positions in a business, which are distant yet powerful. The size of your office; its nearness to top leadership is a defining characteristic of this type of culture.

One of my first jobs in London, in the Engineering field, was as a junior draughtsman (when engineering drawings were done by hand). I worked under a Pakistani prince and an Indian with a Civil Engineering Doctorate.

On the face of it, the class conflict between the two is problematic—taking into consideration their culture clash (Muslim versus Hindu). One had been born to wealth and privilege while the other had earned his position of wealth and privilege.

Our "superior" was a white man who had no idea of the complicated relationship between the two—which added to the fact that they were both suffering from Culture Shock, having to make their way in the cold damp weather and culture of England.

I was witness to daily arguments that would explode at the most innocent of comments from one or the other; even as their clashes were exacerbated by the "superior" white man, who would act like some colonial judge adjudicating "the natives." The ultimate power he wielded was to invoke the "head office" and the ramifications that would result if the behavior of the engineers were to be reported.

You see, shame and blame are handy tools for controlling people with a lot of pride. Earning status and power in the pyramid business structure is based on knowing your place and performing within the job classification that has been assigned to you.

My American example of the pyramid business culture has been referenced in my essay "Coming to America":

> *My first encounter with Americana came after I pounded the streets for a month, looking for a position comparable to that of an Engineer, which I'd been in London. I was told by an agency interviewer, in no uncertain terms, that as a Black man I could not hope to get a position that would allow for upward mobility. I could only hope for lateral movement.*

Status, I was to quickly learn in America, was based on race; and because I was Black, private industry was going to be out of bounds for me, unless I could form my own company.

The project-based business structure is related, in my experiences, to the non-profit world. I've worked in the art (poetry) sector and the education sector, and while the administrators of these non-profits run them like corporations— in a patriarchal manner—there is a lot of turn-over of friendly people who bring incredible talents and energy to their projects, but who are never fully rewarded.

Non-profit, by nature, is based on the financial reality that the organization is spending money it doesn't earn; at the same time, the organization is held accountable for documenting the minutiae of every single act of the organization for review by also overworked government officials.

And this is a good thing and could and should lead to people realizing that they can do better creating, deciding and being accountable to themselves for how their energies are spent.

Project-based businesses have also morphed into contract workers who are employed to do a specific service only, and they are paid off, with no ownership of the final product. Many online "jobs" are using this model now, which spares the entities employing these workers from any tax responsibilities nor any societal responsibility for creating dignity in work that captures and engages human-beings.

I worked as an extra on a movie for a few weeks, and I can honestly say that it was one of the worst experiences I've ever had in the pursuit of making money. To begin with, the money is nothing and is subjected to every tax imaginable. Secondly, the money was earned sitting around, late at night, and sometimes into the early hours of the morning, freezing my balls off.

It was in the Oakland Coliseum, a film version of a fascinating book by Michael Lewis. I'd read the book and thought it would be "cute" to be involved in a movie (the California dream that draws people here is to be in a movie—and that's why Californians act all the time like they're in a movie!).

My co-extras were all bedazzled by the movies, and many were professional extras. I was amazed to learn that many people hovered on the edge of the movie industry for years, without any lines or credits.

When I became the free therapy agent regarding their personal lives, I realized why "reality TV" is so favorite—because the TMZ producers will never run out of material. Project business, for others, was the nearest I've come to be a modern day indentured servant. I was fed peanuts and seduced by the silver screen into suspending my disbelief in how little I mattered.

When I worked for myself, creating video poetry projects, presenting poetry slams, videoing construction projects, and writing books, the sense of worth and reward was second to none—still is. Every time I finish a project, I wonder why I ever allowed myself to succumb to working for others.

Because when I work for others, they never appreciate what I am bringing them. The most effective management tool for keeping workers happy is just to say thank you. It doesn't cost a dime, yet it's worth a million dollars to those who put their hearts, bodies, and souls into their work. Yet most managers and owners do everything but show appreciation.

That is why I like working on my own projects, regardless of how much (or how little) money I make.

The start-up is the new kid on the block, and its focus is on creativity and growth. The casual internal business structure and small groups focus on projects that coordinate with an overall company development, making the start-up an ideal setting for young people getting their feet wet in a business environment.

However, I don't have any specific experience with this business structure because I'm not a nerd. But, given that I'm a social psychologist of sorts (I see myself as having made a life-long personal study of human behavior in cultural settings—a contemporary anthropologist), what strikes me the most about the people who get into start-ups is their lack of social skills and their correspondingly top-heavy faith in technology.

Like an engineer whose primary skills are in designing roads, technologists act on and promote their expertise above others—rather than expanding their knowledge of the human side—because technology comes more easily to them. Most engineers I've met in more than thirty years in and around the industry have no idea how people outside of their sector think or feel, or even how people think and feel generally.

I think of engineers as surrogate Englishmen—in the absence of a personal emotional intelligence system, they document, quantify and value everything by the numbers. American whites are like that, too, though less so.

The final business culture is that of government, where status is achieved by one's position on an organizational chart. I worked for twenty years in several Public Works departments in the Bay Area. I can admit that my reasons for taking such a position—which I disliked—were for expediency's sake. I had a young family and was new to the country and needed to have a stable income.

Americans have reasonable cause to be suspicious of government, but not for the usual reasons of blame and shame that all the libertarians present (until they are in government positions and realize that, without government, American would quickly collapse into anarchy within a month).

No, the problem with government is not the government but the people who inhabit the positions within the government. Except for the more senior and exotic business positions, most of the people who do the grunt work, are under-appreciated, underpaid and soon become bitter. When you go to a window at the post office or call the IRS or apply for social security, you're not talking to a happy worker protecting the integrity of liberal, fair and honest government. No, you're talking to someone who's not making nearly enough money to keep body and soul together, someone who's bullied and unappreciated by his or her higher paid supervisors, who do less and less work as they move up the organizational ladder.

The person you're dealing with began his or her career proud to serve people and happy to have a stable job after a two-year obstacle course of a vetting and interview process. So, it's important to remember one is dealing with a human being who has suffered for the privilege of working for the government.

Government is the only thing that separates us from the barbarity of the "human market place." And if you doubt me, go and live in a third world environment for a year. I challenge any American to set up a business in an environment without the rule of law. Because the private industry does not establish and maintain the rule of law in parts of the world where there is no government.

The transportation system, economic system, banking system, health system, military system, energy system, education system, and technology system are all supported by our government, and we have seen, even with government support, that big business still doesn't do its share in helping to bring the whole country up, as they take every advance—

provided by the stability created by government—to increase their own profits.

The culture of government has not even the veneer of respectability now as it is being subjected to lay-offs and efficiency programs and nastier and nastier career-climbing managers who care for nothing outside of their pension plans and developing elaborate schemes to pass the buck onto their subordinates while undermining, at every chance, their superiors. When I worked for the government, I was always amazed at the end of the year how anything ever got done.

I WILL SURVIVE

Yellow dots of light reflect
off the ink-black lake.
Oily & petrified
the skin of darkness covers the flavor
of my festering anxieties.
Like yeast rising
my fumes pace through me
suspending waves of impermanence.
The chill wet mist tastes of
beechwood as I search for
a Certainty—
a path back that goes forward
to my life in the now.
Where cloves smell of Jasmine broiled in coconut.

Bloody-minded anxiety
dissolves childish splashes
of brightness, running wild
a frightened child engineers frustration,
as algae congeal in oily blackness.

Respect is earned not given!
A departing father says to his son.
This life is bunk, not evil—
live by your own law—you'll learn!
Finally,
exasperation passes.
My disquietude stoops
coated with the ether of equanimity,
scented with misted almonds
sluicing across the lake sky
in the fluttering dawn

STEP EIGHT – HOW TO GIVE A SPEECH

To be effective in public speaking, it's vital to bear in mind some basic principles:

- Get people's attention.
- Welcome them.
- Introduce yourself.
- State the purpose of your presentation.
- State how you want to deal with questions.

1. THERE ARE SEVERAL WAYS TO GET PEOPLE'S ATTENTION:
- If I could have everybody's attention.
- If we can start.
- Perhaps we should begin?
- Let's get started.

2. INTRODUCTION:
- Welcome to Successful Thinkers Network.
- Thank you for coming today.
- Good morning, ladies and gentlemen.
- On behalf of *Moore Consulting*, I'd like to welcome you.

3. INTRODUCE YOURSELF:
- My name is Ian Moore. I'm responsible for travel arrangements.
- For those of you who don't know me, my name is Ian. Moore.
- As you know, I oversee public relations.
- I am a new teacher.

4. STATE THE PURPOSE OF YOUR PRESENTATION:
- This morning I'd like to present my new program.
- Today I'd like to discuss how to be a successful speaker.

- This afternoon, I'd like to report on my Job Success seminar.

5. *STATE HOW YOU WANT TO DEAL WITH QUESTIONS:*
    - If you have any questions, I'll be happy to answer them as we go along.
    - Feel free to ask any questions.
    - Perhaps we can leave any questions you have until the end?
    - There will be plenty of time for questions at the end.

Of course, these are only suggestions, and another language is possible. Even within this limited group of phrases, just choose a few you feel comfortable with and learn and use those.

The importance of public speaking was a critical part of my acculturation into America because it forced me to get out into the community and share my ideas. One of the things that happen when you speak out is that you get feedback from friends, co-workers and those who disagree with what you have to say.

I learned a lot. Not only about how to articulate my ideas, but also how those ideas affected others, and sometimes how they created opposition. You cannot please everyone all the time, or even some of the time, but that doesn't mean you don't speak what's on your mind. That's how we learn, after all.

For me, learning public speaking and joining networking groups, who encouraged me to speak (such as Toastmasters, Business Networking International, and Successful Thinkers Network) allowed me to practice, in a supportive environment so I could improve my message about my work—I'm a self-employed communications consultant specializing in ESL, Job Readiness and Acculturation into America—and attract attention from those who would want my services.

I realized, when I joined these groups, how important it is to develop an Elevator Speech, one that introduces you and your experience and service in less than 40 seconds. My programs provide support and encouragement for people new to America, also those who have not had the opportunity to develop these skills.

Here is a speech I gave about why I write, to my Successful Thinkers Networking group.

SPREADING THE DISEASE OF LITERATURE

Picture this…you've finished the final draft of your manuscript and sent it off to your publisher for final proofreading and publication. You sit back in your chair and look through the Contents page of your book and relive the stories, experiences, and efforts that have filled up the last year of your every free hour. Your partner comes into your writing room with a bottle of champagne and two glasses and gives you a great big hug and toasts your success.

Wrapped in supportive arms, you realize that you've done it. You've fulfilled a dream that you've had for years. You have the living proof that your passion has a beginning, a middle, and an end. All these ideas are manifested in this book. You now have credibility in your world!

Hi, I am Ian Moore, Published Writer, Teacher, and Career Consultant. I've written several books of non-fiction, poetry, short stories—and a novel I just published that took me 20 years to write.

My passion is Literature. I absolutely love words, and ideas, and stories. I'm a fanatical reader and a mad collector of books. I'm here today to infect you with the disease of literature. I intend to stimulate your passion for writing your story. I want you to experience the euphoria of having your name on the sleeve of a book and see the eyes of your buyers' water with admiration at his accomplishment. Because every thinking person wants the world to know that he or she has a story worthy of sharing.

I didn't always have this love of literature. In my early years, I was a sports jock and loved to play soccer, rugby and cricket. Violent and competitive sports were what I learned in my British boarding school, where I was a resident for ten years. If you've read or seen, Charles Dickens' story, "Oliver Twist" you will get an idea of how barbaric public education for orphans was and still is in many parts of Britain. A decade is a long time to be incarcerated in an institution, and when one is young, it can be crippling.

In most cases, people don't recover from the disconnect from family life. I was lucky to be encouraged by one of my teachers, who told me to stop wasting my talents in the sports fields and use them to enlighten and educate myself. Which I proceeded to do.

But my real liberation came through travel. And like Christine (or anyone who has thrown off the yoke of his or her home country and gone exploring), I found that traveling can be a very liberating experience. For traveling not only introduces you to another country, but it also introduces you to yourself, from another perspective. You soon learn that there are lots of yous, and the more you travel, the more you discover about yourself.

After thirteen years traveling in Britain, Europe, the Middle East, North, and West Africa, I came to America; and from the time of my early travels, I kept a diary. When I read those first scribblings, they seem full of despair and bitterness. I didn't think much about them, but I kept scribbling.

When I came to America, I used to talk to my new friends about my experiences visiting other countries. I was surprised to find that many people in California had not traveled anywhere, except on tourist trips. In Europe, everyone travels. Many of my new friends urged me to write my stories down. At first, I didn't think anyone would be interested in them. But after my story-telling began irritating my wife, she told me to write them down because she was sick of hearing about them.

So, I began writing them down.

My first efforts at writing were essays describing my experiences places I visited. This is probably the easiest way to start writing for anyone. Just write down in simple language how you felt when you were in those new places. Fill the story out with incidents that were memorable to you.

I published my first book by hand, selecting the paper and printing every page out on my computer. I designed and formatted the cover, getting the ISBN number and registering it with the Library of Congress. It was a passionate endeavor that took me many months of writing, editing, formatting and standing over my printer and willing it not to destroy the special paper that I'd spent a fortune buying. Finally, it was completed, and I was exhausted.

I decided that I would never do that again. So I spent another small fortune on Vanity Press publishers (these are the publishers that make you pay all the expenses to have your book published, plus their profit). As you all probably know, when you have a passion for something, you don't care about the expense because you're convinced that providence will see you through. So, despite spending my child's college fund, I was encouraged to continue writing, which was all that I was really interested in. Sometimes your passion takes total control of you, and you find yourself becoming a writer-holic.

So, over the past twenty years I've learned a lot about the publishing industry, the good and the bad. Yet I'm even more passionate about writing, and as I mentioned earlier, I've just finished a novel I've been working on for all that time. It's called *I Dream America* and is about a young Ghanaian woman, who journeys to America to find the husband who disappeared three years before and gets swept up in the underbelly of American life in the early 1990s. She struggles with the new world environment and her own self-discovery as she searches for and finds her husband and restores him to health and sanity.

The wonderful reassurance I find about literature, particularly in today's world where people are addicted to distractions and the immediacy of trivia, is that literature teaches the skills of concentration and reflection. Skills that are essential for living a full and meaningful life. As the philosopher, Socrates stated, "An unexamined life is a life not worth living."

And we who come to the Successful Thinkers Network come to examine our lives and make them more meaningful.

That's why we're here. Everyone here should, therefore, be writing his or her story, for it's a way to validate your experiences, share your knowledge and establish credibility in your craft or business. Nothing says success about a person than when a person has published a book. It spells out his or her gift to the world.

I would like to share with you the three habits of writers:
1) Reading (This is the most important. If you don't read you're not practiced in thinking. To write, you must read and think before you can put pen to paper or finger to keypad.)
2) Writing daily (Diaries, notebooks—just imagine you're writing to your grandma.)
3) Reviewing, re-writing, and improving (*The Elements of Style* by E.B. White is an excellent resource during the editing process.)

As Ernest Hemingway always said:
"*A writer must write what he has to say, not speak it.*

I'M A WRITER-HOLIC

Hi, I'm Ian, and I'm a writer-holic.
I wasn't always this way, I was raised
with a slate and chalk. I only started
using pen and ink when I was thirteen.
In High School and College, they **forced me** to
use a computer, but I resisted.
Recently I lost my job and my dream
of making a living without writing
collapsed. I just could not help myself.
I started writing uncontrollably.
From first thing in the morning 'til late night,
I wrote feverishly as if my life were
dependent on my words, poems and stories!
Now I've lost my friends and family
—Doctor, what can I do?

STEP NINE – TOMORROW BELONGS TO THE COMMUNICATORS

- Are you a student or professional who recognizes the need for improvement in your presentation and speech?
- Are you a business leader who recognizes the need for speech improvement in your employees?
- Are you an individual who recognizes that you will make more progress and money in your career when you communicate better?

Speech coaching picks up where ESL classes stop. Improving your ability to communicate in English is of growing importance to business professionals developing new enterprises or advancing in corporate America.

SPEECH COACHING OFFERS THE FOLLOWING BENEFITS:
- Breathing and exercises that make speaking effortless and commanding
- The proper placement of tongue, lips, and teeth
- The placement of the accent on the correct syllable
- Hearing and practicing the appropriate consonant sounds and the special rules that apply to English
- Learning the proper vowel sounds, both long and short

By developing awareness about how sounds in English are formed, you will be able to reproduce them and learn practical exercises that will remind you of your challenges and how to overcome them.

WORKING WITH A SPEECH COACH WILL GIVE YOU PRACTICAL EXERCISES:

- That will show you how to articulate diphthongs
- For use with voiced and unvoiced consonants and sounds
- That will develop your feel for English rhythms
- To teach you to slow down, speak within one breath at a time, which will improve your pacing, tone and pitch
- For developing listening skills
- About business etiquette for professionals
- To help you learn basic English grammar
- Focused on the correct usage of idiomatic and colloquial expressions in formal or casual settings
- That explain the nuances of American culture

It's not a speech coach's intention to eliminate your accent, but by becoming aware of the distinct sounds and physical challenges you have in speaking English, you will learn to be understood clearly and intelligently by native speakers of English. At the same time, you will retain the appealing aspects of your native language that make you unique.

The speech coach programs I offer include a workbook specifically designed for you. The book contains:

- Pronunciation drills
- Tongue twisters
- Breathing exercises
- Poems and Shakespearean reading exercises

- Business telephone etiquette exercises
- Basic English tasks
- Entrepreneurial programs for business start-ups
- Business English for executives

For success in learning the nuances of English, I recommend that students take classes twice a week for a minimum of a month. Additional time needed will be determined by the speech coach and the client. It's also essential to practice every day. The workbook will provide you with daily exercises.

All students will be video/audiotaped at the beginning of the lesson programs and at the end of the time set to achieve their goals. Each student will receive a copy of before and after video/audio recordings. They will also get to keep the workbook as a constant reminder of their ongoing education.

As a native English speaker, from London, England, I bring to my students 40 years of sharing my love of the English language with many people from around the world. I've lived and worked in England, Scotland, France, Spain, Greece, Turkey, Israel, Algeria, Ghana, Cote d'Ivoire, Sierra Leone, Jamaica, Cuba, Canada, the USA, and China. Throughout my travels, I've always been fascinated by the cultural exchange that goes on when you are open to listen, feel and share other people's ideas.

STEP TEN – THE CULTURE OF SURVIVAL

When I first arrived in Oakland, California, I was overwhelmed with the new environment. I had read about Oakland while in Britain and had discovered that it was the most integrated city in America at the time, during the 1980s. The term didn't mean a lot to me because I had been integrated into the British world where I was born. Plus I'd lived in other European and West African countries and learned that people have similar issues but often different ways of resolving them.

Oakland was the home of the Pointer Sisters, whom I adored, and The Black Panthers whose defiant stance was the catalyst that put the first Black mayor of Oakland into office, setting in motion the changing of the guard in terms of facial color for those in political office. (Political power, I learned in West Africa, doesn't have a color, except green.) My first wife was a foot-soldier in the Panthers, as were a lot of the blacks I met when I first arrived in Oakland.

But the Panthers left a divisive history behind them in the Oakland community; half the people I met talked about them as just another street gang that read philosophy books while others praised them for giving black people the courage to stand up to the white man.

Armed with a European sensibility—and not susceptible to the triggers of American prejudices—I found myself living among the black middle-class of Oakland. All the people I met during my first six months were professional people with good jobs and homes and families. The beautiful Mediterranean weather, the variety of beautiful people, the casual friendliness and the philosophy of Black America were poured into me over those initial months of acculturation.

It wasn't all peaches, as I've discussed in my other writings, but what I learned from the black community was how to survive. The American dream, to most black professionals, was to get a government job and build your own business on the side. But, above all else, the American dream meant personal freedom and Integrity to me, and I was determined—having now escaped the class system of Britain—to live my life by my beliefs.

My first job was as a custodian at San Francisco City College, where I cleaned classrooms and bathrooms at night and went to school during the day—taking a full load of engineering classes. My wife was ashamed of my job, having married me for the glamour that she thought would come to her because of my English pedigree.

The precociousness of my wife's daughter, who blamed me for her absent father, overwhelmed me as I stepped unwittingly into an alien world with few friends to guide me. For five years I lived in the shadows; working nights, sleeping in the days and trying to make sense of a family life that exposed me to the trivia and nastiness of selfish black shallow people. One day I walked away from it all.

I had finally found myself a government job in the engineering field. My wife, who only wanted to work part-time for a charity program, had given up all pretense of being my partner even though it was my money and work that were supporting her and her daughter. I achieved that government job over eighteen months without any family or community support, during which I had to travel around the Bay Area, always to undesirable locations where I had to to take tests that ranged in duration from one to four hours.

Meanwhile, I continued to work as a custodian and was subjected to random acts of spite and envy from my black supervisors for daring to question them. The majority of the custodians I worked with at City College and later at City Hall, in San Francisco, were immigrants from Central America, the Philippines, and China, many of them had Ph.D.'s from their own countries but unable to speak English denied them the opportunities to get a comparable job in America. I was on good terms with everyone there, except the Black supervisors. I tried to encourage my fellow workers when I was left, to fulfill their American dream.

My educational efforts had provided me with an AA degree in Civil Engineering, and I began working in the Oakland Public Works Department as a construction inspector. I patrolled East Oakland and met many unique black characters.

This was the time when Felix Mitchell's drug activities dominated the areas around 82nd and 90th avenues. I never had any conflicts with his gang—I didn't act like a cop—and interestingly, as a black government worker, I received a lot of respect from the predominately black community. I had the most challenging time with the politically connected black homeowners who were friends with the mayor. These conflicts brought retributions down on my head from my supervisors—which I resisted because I genuinely believed I was working for the public good and I was proud of that fact.

After a few years, I was recruited by a black man to work for the county. That's when I was made aware of the title HNC (Head Nigger in Charge). This supervisor owned me or acted as if he did. I'd never been exposed to black on black conflict before; as a result, I didn't play his game. This left me vulnerable to racist attacks from most white supervisors who didn't want me in the job in the first place.

So, after my first two positive probationary reports in the first six months, my two white supervisors returned blatantly biased adverse reports and tried to shaft me on my third report. My HNC hung me out to dry. I was alone against a patronage system that traditionally provided Public Works jobs to the white alumni of the agency. So, when I was dragged before the head of the department by my racist supervisors, I made sure I prepared myself and launched into a point-by-documented- attack on their lack of support for me, as well as documented incidents during which they contradicted their own earlier reports.

Whether because of the fear of a racial law-suit or because the head of the department knew these two supervisors were incompetent, he exonerated me, gave me a full-time position and demoted and transferred the two supervisors.

That was not the end of the challenges I had to face during the next eleven years working with the government. During that time, I had to be constantly on my guard. I had to always do the best job I could do because I could expect no favors. I put up with racial attacks from both the white and black members of the agency, my fellow-workers as well as my supervisors.

From these personal attacks, I learned that my only security was doing an excellent professional job. And in that spirit, I went back to school and took more classes in engineering. I also learned about video recording, editing, and documentation and developed a program for using video cameras to document the construction process.

My program of video documentation eliminated the human error factor (which was considerable) and was eventually written into the Caltrans specifications for construction projects. Ironically, it was in connection with my greatest success within the government that I was finally undermined for the final time. In hindsight, I realize I was naive and failed to follow the organizational chart protocol, but I'd had such a negative time with the HNC that I took my video idea to the County Engineer.

The County Engineer loved my idea but referred me back to the HNC, who relished the opportunity to kill the project. As a result, I gave up on any hope that people in government had any integrity or business sense. And one day I walked away from it. I left behind a pension, unemployment pay, and an easy job because it was killing my soul every minute of every day that I worked there.

It was a hard transition to the private sector. It was even harder explaining my stubbornness to my new wife and child who was going to a private school. But I knew that if I were going to make my dream come true, I could not compromise it on the altar of a government pension. America had allowed me to live a life of freedom and that meant, to me, living a life of integrity.

I was 48 years old, and I had many productive years ahead of me which, I am sad to say the government didn't need. So I set about challenging myself as I began to learn in real time that if I wanted something in this life 1)I must clearly define my goal; 2) create a plan that allowed me to measure my progress towards that goal; and 3), if my actions and results don't meet with my goals, expectations, and success, I must do something else!

One thing that stands out, as I look back at my early years in America, was that every time I stood up to racists and cowards and liars and cheats and weak manipulating people, my next job, position or opportunity was exponentially better. I made more money, worked in a better environment and learned more about my capacity to succeed.

One manifestation of this new confidence was that I became a video poet, producing award-winning national videos and helping to run a national video festival for more than five years. This experience gave me the confidence to develop my own cable show: Culture Shock News. The documented interviews in Part II of my culture shock book were the first show, broadcast in San Francisco. Later, throughout the 1990s, I established a weekly cable program that was broadcast throughout the Bay Area, from Livermore to Marin, to San Francisco, to Oakland and San Jose.

It never made me rich, but it was a work of love exploring the themes that I've outlined in my writings. However, it was yet another example of how in America one can gain access to all kinds of creative outlets—if you're prepared to do the work. The culmination of this interest was in working on a poetry program that featured Maya Angelou.

Throughout the 2000s I worked for myself, as a contract construction inspector, using my video documentation skills. I wrote six books and self-published them during that time, exploring the publishing and writing industry, which had me traveling all around America and to the Caribbean. I dipped back into working for the government—a terrible mistake—just as the economy collapsed, and I joined everyone else running for cover, spending the next five years climbing out from a pit caused by the excess of the American dream and the government's abandonment of its responsibilities.

"A person often meets his destiny on the road he took to avoid it." (Jean de La Fontaine) And so it was for me as I was buttressed between government relief programs and my personal pride to find employment in the newly burgeoning solar industry, but where I found only that I was now a victim of age discrimination.

From a poetic perspective, I could appreciate how I'd now encompassed all the prejudices on display in America. I could add to my badges of discrimination that of the immigrant, the Brit, the Black, the brown, the nigga, the wog, the mulatto, the bastard, the legal alien, the arrogant, the self-righteous, and now the senior citizen.

I can't think of anywhere else in the world where I could amass associations with so many stereotypes. But signing up for a senior citizen program, I had the opportunity to talk myself into being a career coach. My experiences had given me plenty of stories to tell and plenty of examples of what it takes to survive in Europe, Africa and the United States of America. So, I fashioned a program from my experiences and studies for my fellow senior citizens.

My success at creating and presenting a career coaching program encouraged me to challenge myself once more: I found that many senior citizens, and indeed many people I met in Oakland, needed to learn English speaking skills. I, therefore, signed up for an online ESL class, while at the same time volunteering at the English Center in Oakland. It was at the English Center that I learned the practical skills of teaching ESL. Within a year I was confident enough to seek employment at several non-profit organizations looking for someone who could come in and develop and administer an ESL program for several their residences.

Teaching ESL led to a computer class, and GED classes, and soon I was working as a contract teacher all around the Bay Area. It was while studying, researching, teaching and developing these programs that I discovered that I truly loved teaching. I realized that after all the years I'd tried to push myself into a square hole, I was really a round peg!

An essential ingredient that helped me survive in America turned out to be my discussions with black men. People my age, in Oakland, had been through the Black Panther years and the experiences of having to survive under challenging circumstances than black people today. Their stories happened before the drug epidemic in the black community, which has affected every family and turned traditional black family values upside down.

My first wife's family had all been raised to get a job and spurn welfare as an evil of laziness. By the 1990s many black middle-class families had been devastated by drugs and gang warfare. White families and commentators despise the statistics of the black community as if all the black people in the black community chose to take drugs and steal and avoid working—when there were and still are institutional and societal obstacles impeding the progress of the collective black community even to this day.

My real education, then, came from these brothers who had been to war—in Vietnam and on the streets of Oakland—and their stories were ones of learning to think on one's feet, to confront problems with a mind to solving them, to take responsibility for oneself, and to understand that the only one who can save you is you.

These individuals didn't hide behind the church or government or the rose-tinted glasses of the white man's "house on the hill." They knew from experience that, they were born in America and their ancestors had cultivated and created value and wealth in America.

My new-found-friends were still considered second-class citizens, like myself, but they earned what they got in their hands daily. My experiences on the roads of Europe and Africa had also taught me these truths "…that a real individual is measured only by the effort he or she puts into taking full responsibility for his or her actions."

I believe that you cannot be an honest and free individual unless you can stand alone, taking responsibility for yourself! When I left England to come to America, I, like many others, took up that mantle of true freedom, and it is what informs me today as I challenge myself to give of my best effort and continue to improve myself. And because I have this commitment, which I cultivated for many years, I'm now in the position to accept the responsibility of being a teacher.

Because to teach, you must be able to focus on the needs of your students, provide them with encouragement and model for them the freedom to think creatively, without bringing your own problems into the equation.

In thirty years of living in California, I've fashioned 7 essential steps to surviving here in the United States:

1) *GIVE UP USING CREDIT.* What this means is this: Don't go into debt—because the only way American society keeps

its citizens passive is through debt. When you accept credit, your creditor knows you will go into debt and is happy to feed your addiction. Credit says that you cannot live within your means. There are many free products, services, and programs in California that provide all of the basics for healthy, comfortable living. Credit says you want more than you deserve and is the chain that will enslave you for the rest of your life if you let it.

2) *BE YOUR OWN HEALTH GUIDE.* More than 190,000 people enter American hospitals every year and die because of an incorrect diagnosis. The cost of being ill is hazardous to your health, literally. The health industry is the only industry that operates outside of the capitalist system. Doctors are not rewarded for doing a good job. (I once told my doctor that I would only pay him when I was well and would stop paying him the moment I became ill, thereby giving him an incentive to cure me!) They get paid whether you're well or ill.

The health industry, which is dominated by attorneys who fix premiums and payments for health care procedures, also gets to write the laws that govern them and their pay while drug companies bribe doctors to promote their drugs. Now that's what is called a real drug dealer! With the information freely available online and through countless personal stories beamed to us daily through the media, there is no reason why anyone should not be able to monitor and maintain a healthy lifestyle free from all but the deadliest illnesses through responsible self-healing.

3) *DON'T BELIEVE ANYTHING YOU HEAR OR SEE ON TV OR SOCIAL MEDIA, WITHOUT THREE INDEPENDENT CONFIRMATIONS.* You will tell me that you have no time to

do this, and I will tell you that the time it takes to check the source for honesty will be less than the time you lose in recouping the money you will lose chasing after a stupid idea. If the people who parade themselves on Court TV, believing that they've gained celebrity-hood by being silly in public (the most stupid cases are picked for their entertainment value, not proper justice!), stopped to think about the time, reputation and money they've lost, they would be better off paying off whoever they've offended and moved on.

Concerning technology and our nation's manic obsession with new gadgets, I'm reminded of what Neil Postman identified in his books *Technopoly* and *Amusing Ourselves to Death*, when it comes to how we should view technology and society, we should ask the following questions before casting our vote or wasting our money:

a) What is the problem that the particular technology is solving?
b) Whose problem is it? Who will benefit and who will pay?
c) If we solve the problem, what other problems will be created?
d) Who might be most seriously harmed by the new technology?
e) What changes in language are created by the new technology, and what is gained or lost?
f) What sort of people and institutions acquire economic and political power because of these technological changes?

4) *PRACTICE COMPASSION AND CHARITY EVERY DAY*. I've never met an individual racist American. (In large groups of Americans hatred comes out—it's as if people in groups

try to outdo each other with their hatred.) As individuals, the Americans I've met have been curious about my accent . And giving me time to explain myself. But Americans ultimately want you to be like them and be consumed by what others think of them.

5) *INVEST ONLY IN THE PEOPLE, IDEAS AND THINGS YOU KNOW (INCLUDING YOURSELF).* Three-quarters of the stock market is dominated by big investors. If you cannot afford to invest and lose $50 million, then you're wasting your time. It's true that you can get lucky and make the odd $20,000 scoop (but gamblers quickly forget their losses, which over the year would be double that one lucky strike!), but to be lucky you need to be in the market for ten years or more and/or get a tip from an insider.

Ten percent returns are enormous in the stock market today, but that percentage is not going to give much return on your $10,000 or $100,000 "investment," which will be tied up until your stocks turn around. More importantly, the stock market has become a casino, which it was never meant to be. Gambling is legal in every state but two; there are plenty of ways you can throw your money away. So, if it's gambling you want, you don't need to bother with the stock market!

The stock market was initially developed to invest in capital products and services, such as machines, education, health, and the future of the country—our kids! So, if you want to invest in America, give your money to some young entrepreneur who has a business plan and a product and services that offer more than getting people to click on a button for an unsatisfactory reward. Invest in those who have produced a better mousetrap or the next big thing that will solve some of our country's real problems, improving relationships between cultures, helping to heal the epidemic of loneliness and poverty in America, and encouraging people to take a more active role in the governance of the country.

6) *KNOW YOUR RIGHTS & RESPONSIBILITIES*. Study the American Constitution and understand how we got here and how precariously the early settlers held onto life, liberty and the pursuit of happiness. Nothing is a given. Every immigrant coming to this country has terrifying stories about how his or her life was once, upon a time, balanced and peaceful in the home country, until an Earthquake, Typhoon, Massacre, War, or Health Epidemic swept their land and homes away.

Even in this country, every year the mid-west is hit by tornadoes that destroy a lifetime of memories. In the East winter storms grow more significant and deadlier every year, creating real disasters that movies cannot even pretend to duplicate in their story-telling. These disasters are not God's will or punishment for the wrong political beliefs; there is nothing the victims did to cause these problems.

We have real problems daily in America that need practical solutions from thinking, caring people. We in America cannot hide behind our smartphones and internet gadgets believing that all will be well because we want it to be so. Disaster can and does strike without warning, and spending a trillion dollars on our military, or filling our homes with guns will not stop the moment when it comes. The only protection from uncertainty in knowledge, reason, and understanding about the mechanisms of social order and finding consensus with our neighbors as to how to solve our problems together so that everyone benefits.

7) *NEVER, EVER, EVER GIVE UP!* America is a place where eventually you'll get what you deserve, but you must keep working and challenging yourself. The political, religious and social restrictions that happen to most people in other cultures around the world have little or no effect here in America; indeed there is a glass ceiling in all phases of life, but if you want to dedicate yourself to breaking through the glass ceiling, then it's up to you to make an effort—and you'll be joining ranks with individuals and groups who changed the way Americans work because of their efforts.

However, to keep developing and improving your life, you must keep your brain working efficiently. You can do this by reading and thinking about self-improvement. The bookstores and internet are full of self-improvement advice; it's your challenge to find the information that will help you on your road to success.

As a teacher of math, I'm always asked by adults who are taking their GED, "Why should I study math?" They tell me they can add and subtract, divide and multiply, so why do they need algebra? I demonstrate with riddles and games that the brain is just a muscle, and just as with the muscles in your legs or arms, you wouldn't suddenly get up from your office chair and sprint around a track; so too with your brain; algebra is one of the ways you can exercise your brain.

Your brain is a muscle that needs to be exercised; math exercises the brain. Math teaches you how to think, not what to think. In short, we need to practice and exercise our thinking brains if we want them to work efficiently. Therefore, social science is so important; it presents us—unlike math—with open questions and a wide variety of answers to any given issue, requiring that we have a full breadth of knowledge about the subject so that all the stakeholders are included in a solution.

LET AMERICA BE AMERICA AGAIN
by Langston Hughes

Let America be America again.
Let it be the dream it used to be.
Let it be the pioneer on the plain
Seeking a home where he himself is free.

(America never was America to me.)

Let America be the dream the dreamers dreamed—
Let it be the great strong land of love
Where never Kings connive nor tyrants scheme
That any man be crushed by one above.

(It never was America to me.)

O, let my land be a land where Liberty
Is crowned with no false patriotic wreath,
But opportunity is real, and life is free,
Equality is in the air we breathe.

(There's never been equality for me, or freedom in this homeland of the free.)

Say who are you that mumbles in the dark?
And who are you that draws your veil across the stars?

Me, I'm the poor white, fooled and pushed apart,
I am the Negro bearing slavery's scars.
I am the Red man driven from the land,
I am the immigrant clutching the hope I seek—
And finding only the same old stupid plan
Of dog eat dog, of mighty crush the weak.

I am the young man, full of strength and hope,
Tangled in that ancient endless chain
Of profit, power, gain, of grab the land!
Of grab the gold! Of grab the ways of satisfying need!
Of work the men! Of take the pay!
Of owning everything for one's own greed!

I am the farmer, bondsman to the soil.
I am the worker sold to the machine.
I am the Negro, servant to you all.
I am the people, worried, hungry, mean—
Hungry yet today despite the dream;
Beaten yet today—O, Pioneers!
I am the man who never got ahead,
The poorest worker bartered throughout the years.

Yet I'm the one who dreamt our basic dream
In that Old World while still a serf of Kings,
Who dreamt a dream so strong, so brave, so true,
That even yet its mighty daring sings
In every brick and stone, in every furrow turned
That's made America the land it has become.
O, I'm the man who sailed those early seas
In search of what I meant to be my home—
For I'm the one who left dark Ireland's shore,
And Poland's plain, and England's grassy lea,
And torn from Black Africa's strand I came
To build a "homeland of the free."

The Free?

A dream—still beckoning to me!
O, Let America be America again—
The Land that never has been yet—
And yet must be—

The land where every man is free.
The land that's mine
The poor man's, Indian's, Negro's, ME—
Who made America,
Whose sweat and blood, whose faith and pain,
Whose hands at the foundry, whose plow in the rain,
Must bring back our mighty dream again.

Sure, call me any ugly name you choose –
The steel of freedom does not stain.
From those who live like leeches on the people's lives,
We must take back our land again,
America!
O, yes,
I say it plain, America never was America to me.
We the people, must redeem
Our land, the mines, the plants, the rivers,
The mountains and the endless plain—
And all, all the stretch of these great green states—
And make America again!

YouTube video: "Let America Be America Again"
https://www.youtube.com/watch?v=Xhvsa279QgQ

ABOUT THE AUTHOR: IAN C. DAWKINS MOORE

MY BIOSPHERE
My name is Ian, in England born
My father's from the islands, my mum's from that shore
My youth was spent fleeing xenophobic bores.

I traveled to Athens and Timbuktu
I bathed in Alhambra, Granada too
I could never shake my brooding school.

My American wife dragged me here
My stepdaughter in tow, a brand-new sphere
My opposition to the states took five years to clear.

I started again, from scratch in haste
I started to relearn a new verb, chase
I started to learn a new action, waste.

My endeavors were positive though painfully slow
My dues well paid, eventually did grow
My overnight success took many moons to glow.

I now serve the public civil and clean
I now work the markets and international scene
I now have great credit and a labyrinth machine.

My writing before covered prose and essay
My heroes are Baldwin, Soyinka and Sesay
My novel attempts include travel and jazzy.

I read like a fish that swims in the night
I spend more on books than I have such a right
I meditate, cool out, and stay UN-Tight.

My dreams are to learn the heart of the word
My hopes are to chase that winged bird
My endeavors I pray are to teach and be heard.

I live in Oakland, city caught in a lie
I dwell in environs of many colored eyes
I inhabit a space of love and deep sighs.

My time here now is eight years plus
My memories of home are short and cussed
My life's irony is to be an English fuss.

Ian C. Dawkins Moore

WORKSHOPS BY IDMOORECONSULTING
(the *Moore* you Hear, the *Moore* you love)

AVAILABLE ONLINE & LIVE. SKYPE: ICMOORE13

FOR INFORMATION ABOUT PRIVATE AND GROUP PROGRAMS, CONTACT: AMAZDAH3@YAHOO.COM

WORKSHOP #1: PREPARING FOR JOB SEARCH (2 HOURS)
- Self-Assessment and Talent Inventory
- Life Purpose Worksheet
- Assessment of Human Relationship Skills
- Values List

WORKSHOP #2: IMPROVING COMMUNICATIONS (2 HOURS)
- The Three Primary Communication Signals
- Introductory Remarks
- Verbal Communication Signals
- Warm-Up Exercises (breathing, singing, voice exercises)
- Elevator Speeches
- How to Sound Confident
- My Communication Effectiveness

WORKSHOP #3: OVERCOMING BARRIERS (2 HOURS)
- Connections between External and Internal Barriers
- The Elephant's Limits
- External Barriers
- Internal Barriers
- Learning to Overcome Past Challenges
- Strategies for Overcoming Your Fears
- The Four Saboteurs
- Dealing with Change

- Barriers to Employment for the 50+ Job Seeker

WORKSHOP #4: RESUMES & COVER LETTERS (2 HOURS)
- What Is a Resume?
- Human Resources—The Gatekeepers
- Components of a Resume
- Examples of Resumes
- Resume Worksheet
- Examples of Job Descriptions
- Ten Tips to Keep Your Resume Current
- What Is a Cover Letter?
- Types of Cover Letters
- Cover Letter Worksheet
- Purpose of a Resume

WORKSHOP #5: THE INTERVIEW (2 HOURS)
- Interview Preparation (before the interview)
- Researching the Employer
- Information Interviews
- The Stages of an Interview
- Body Language
- What to Do and Not Do
- Types of Interviews
- Common Questions
- Illegal Questions

WORKSHOP #6: PREPARING FOR WORK (2 HOURS)
- What Is Important to Me?
- The ABCs of Job Hunting
- The Rule of Three
- What Kind of Business/Position Do You Really Want?
- Listing 10 Companies Where You Want to Work

- Researching 10 Companies Where You Want to Work

OTHER BOOKS BY IAN C. DAWKINS MOORE

THE RITUALS FOR SUCCESS (2015)
A self-help book with the simple rituals for success: A good diet, exercise and mindfulness about your day ahead, if cultivated, will reward you continuously throughout your days, weeks, months and years to come. This book shares with you the three saboteurs to consistency and success:
One - What frustration teaches us about how we see the world
Two - Why we are so down on ourselves
Three - How we can transform negativity into confidence

THE ARRIVAL (how to survive in America) (2015)
The Arrival tells the story of the 30 years of culture shock experienced by a man of color searching for his place in the New World. Told in tales and poems and anecdotes of acculturation, *The Arrival* embraces all the hopes and aspirations of those who would leave their homes and seek redemption in another land.

The book provides a unique vision of the multifaceted world of America at the end of the twentieth century and the beginning of the twenty-first, offering lessons in survival and the benefits of embracing as your own a vibrant and demanding culture. *The Arrival* reflects 30 years of living and observing life in America and is divided into three parts: Part I – Coming to America, Part II – Living in America; Part III – Surviving in America.

DIVINE PROVIDENCE (2015)
This collection of short stories and poems features "Maili Beach", "Money Balls", "Fake It 'til You Make It", "The

Man Who Wasn't There", "The Vanities of Desire", "Socrates", and more.

THE MEANING OF LIFE (2012)
The Meaning of Life is a collection of short stories and poems of romance, travel and adventure for all readers who love language, words and expression. This collection is dedicated to you and the passionate stories that are now germinating in your hearts. May my humble stories act as a catalyst for your exuberant creations.

RETURN TO MY NATIVE LAND (2008)
As a young man, I traveled in West Africa in search of my identity. I am a man of color who was born in England. I visited West Africa in the mid-seventies before that area exploded into violence and witnessed the displacement of its people. This story is about my encounters with real people in Africa and my personal observations of my time there.

OPEN HEART POETRY (2007)
Open Heart Poetry is iconoclastic poetry, written in a precise language that explores the intricacies of the emotions of love, friendship, and fatherhood, and ruminates on politics, history, music, and the mysteries of life. Each line in every poem explodes with an exact syntax and diction that grips the mind of the reader."
--**Reginald Lockett**, poet and author of "PARTY CRASHERS OF PARADISE"

AMERICA: CULTURE SHOCK (2006)
This book presents the story of culture shock within America to Americans. This book consolidates twenty years of writing and research about my culture shock experience into a

definitive collection of essays, poems, commentaries and stories. They offer practical perspectives for students in high school and college.

GREAT BLACK INNOVATORS & THE PROBLEM-SOLVING PROCESS (2006)
This workbook uses the biographies and historical accomplishments of important black innovators to demonstrate the problem-solving process. The book consists of a six-step program that can be used to resolve any problem.

AFRO-MUSE: THE EVOLUTION OF AFRICAN-AMERICAN MUSIC (2005)
This is the story of music-making in early African societies and its importation to America. The book is a review of the vast amount of research, by others, showing the musical influences from Africa to the Americas. Chapters include "Africa's Musical History", "The Middle Passage", "Seasoning in the Islands", "Conversion to Christianity", "The Spirituals", "The Camp Meetings", "The Blues and Hip-Hop's Origins"

CULTURE SHOCK ESSAYS (1999)
This collection of essays chronicles my travels from England to America and beyond: "Coming to America", "Nice Chap" (about my father), "See London and Die", "Jamaica, No Problem", "China: 6,000 Years in 6 Days", "The Road to Ramadan", "Another Country", "The Promised Land".

Thank you
for taking the time to read my essays.
Please visit
https://www.amazon.com/Ian-C.-Dawkins-Moore/e/B003HETPZ2
for additional information about private & group consultations on
cultural coaching.

All these books are available from
Email: amazdah3@yahoo.com
&
amazon.com, goodreads.com, barnes&noble.com, smashwords.com

Printed in Dunstable, United Kingdom